The Pocket Guide to
Seattle

Duse McLean

Pocket Guide to Seattle

Copyright © 1989 by Duse F. McLean
All rights reserved.

Thistle Press
Bellevue, Washington

Designed by Christina Scholly
Cover illustration by John Schilling
Maps by Andrew McLean
Edited by Allison McLean
Illustrations by E.B. "Pete" McLean

Library of Congress Cataloging-in-Publication
Data

McLean, Duse F.
The pocket guide to Seattle.

Includes index.
1. Seattle, WA, — Description — Guidebooks.
I. Title
88-051967

ISBN 0-9621935-0-X

For information about special purchases
please contact:

  Thistle Press
  P.O. Box 732
  Bellevue, WA 98004

Preface

Seattle is a young city, rich in history—a city known for its beauty and attractive style of life. This small pocket guide is designed to be a convenient reference for discovering and visiting Seattle's many places of interest.

During the past three years, I have worked for the Seattle/King County Convention and Visitors Bureau as a visitor information person. In the course of fielding questions from over 30,000 visitors I noticed a pattern to the queries: They wanted specific answers about what to see, how much attractions cost, hours, and directions. Visitors tend to think in terms of time, such as: "I've got half a day (or a whole day, or three days). What should I see?" Or they think in terms of categories: "What about the harbor tours, or the views, or night life?" They also frequently ask about the necessities: "Where can we eat?" or, the all-time classic, "Where are the restrooms?"

In addition to answering questions for the Convention and Visitors Bureau, I began disseminating information as a tour guide for a convention services company in Seattle. This book is a result of both perspectives— what visitors want to know about Seattle and what there is about Seattle that is interesting.

The Pocket Guide to Seattle is designed to be a succinct, informative reference. It is easy to read, convenient to carry and has pertinent information: hours, cost, phone numbers, and directions for Seattle's attractions. It does not rate or rank attractions, but instead tries to describe places and give enough information so the reader can decide what to visit.

All phone numbers, prices and hours of operation were checked before we went to press. Inevitably, though, some will change, some attractions will cease operation, and others will start up. Always call to verify the information before starting out so you won't be disappointed.

In the course of writing **The Pocket Guide to Seattle** I had help from many sources. My friends and colleagues at the Seattle/King County Convention and Visitors Bureau were full of good ideas and able to keep on top of changing events. The folks at Convention Services Northwest who turned me loose with their valued customers provided me with a whole new perspective of Seattle which I loved. And many people answered questions over the phone or on the job which have become part of this book.

Most of all, my thanks to my family who stood by me as this book went from an idea to the real thing and provided the talent and expertise to produce it. My daughter, Allison, who had the background needed to produce the book; my son Andrew, who designed the maps and helped with photographs for the drawings; Christina Scholly, a talented graphic designer who designed the book and answered many questions throughout its production; my son Alex, a Seattle expert in his own right; and especially my husband, Pete, who read, reread, and helped with every page and, in his spare time, drew the illustrations.

We hope our readers will enjoy Seattle as much as we do.

Table of Contents

Seattle

PART I

Out and About   51

PART II

And More   81

Seattle

Introduction

Seattle is a wonderful city! Its unsurpassed physical setting makes a stunning background for the cosmopolitan city it has become. From its beginning, Seattle has been fortunate to have citizens of vision and strength to create a first-class city. Projects such as rebuilding the city after the Great Fire in 1889, regrading the steep hills in downtown Seattle at the turn of the century, building the locks in 1915, and the World's Fairs of 1909 and 1962 are examples of the "Seattle Spirit," and it is this spirit which has produced the vibrant present-day Seattle.

The first settlers landed on Alki Point in West Seattle in 1861 and moved to Elliott Bay the next spring. They named the city after the Suquamish Indian chief, Sealth, who befriended them. For many years Seattle was known as the "Queen City" because of its dominance in the Northwest. In 1982 the Seattle/King County Convention and Visitors Bureau decided they needed a more contemporary name and sponsored a contest for a new nickname. The winning entry, "The Emerald City" claimed, "Seattle is the jewel of the Northwest, the Queen of the Evergreen State, and is the many-faceted city of space, elegance, magic, and beauty."

Beyond its remarkable physical beauty, Seattle
is probably best known for its climate. The green
lushness is a result of seasonal, usually gentle,
rains brought by Pacific air currents. The resulting
maritime climate keeps Seattle's temperatures
moderate — it rarely freezes or snows in the
winter and days are mild in the summer. Although
it has a reputation for being a rainy city, Seattle's
average annual rainfall is 36 to 38 inches, less
than many East Coast cities. However, the rain
comes in small but frequent amounts. During the
rainy season, November through April, the days
are apt to be dark and damp. Daytime temperatures in the winter months are typically in the 40s
or 50s and seldom drop below freezing. The long
days of the summer months are usually dry and
sunny with high temperatures in the 70s or low
80s. Generally, a raincoat is all that is needed in
winter and a light-weight jacket is a good idea in
the summer.

How to use this guide

This book is organized from the point of view
of someone starting out to see Seattle from downtown; all travel times and distances originate from
central downtown. Hotels and restaurants are not
included, assuming that the reader has already
found a place to stay and will use the resources in
the Other Sources of Information (pages 129-132)
for information about restaurants.

The guide is divided into four major sections;
the first three are by their proximity to downtown
Seattle. Attractions in the "Downtown" section
are easily accessible by public transportation or
walking; the "In and Around" features are a 20 to
30 minute drive from downtown and are accessible by Metro buses; while the "Out and About"
destinations are half-day or longer excursions and
most require a car. The last section, "And More,"
has many categories: ferries, museums and sports,
which are of interest to Seattle residents and

visitors alike. Unless noted, all places are handicapped accessible. Boldfaced items are referenced
in the index.

Please note: We checked all phone numbers
and hours listed in this book for accuracy but
know that inevitably some will change after publi-
cation. Also, some attractions close earlier or do
not operate at all during the winter. **Please call to
verify days and hours of operation when planning your schedule.**

The Pocket Guide includes hundreds of places
in the Greater Seattle area, from the best known to
favorite hideaways. We'd like to know about any
favorites our readers have. Please write to :

Pocket Guide to Seattle
c/o Thistle Press
P.O. Box 732
Bellevue, WA 98004

We hope this book will make seeing Seattle's
sights an enjoyable experience.

GETTING AROUND:

Seattle's downtown is an area about three
miles long confined by Elliott Bay on the west
and I-5 to the east; the Kingdome on King Street
marks the boundary on the south and Seattle Center on Broad Street on the north. Within this small
area are the major business buildings, hotels, and
shops, including Pioneer Square and the venerable
Pike Place Market. Metro buses are free downtown between 4am and 9pm, providing a perfect
way to sightsee.

"Avenues" run parallel to the waterfront,
roughly north and south, and are fairly level;
"Streets" run east and west, up the hills. The basic
number-grid system extends throughout the
greater Seattle area.

The best way to see downtown Seattle is by
walking—that way, you can pause to see the

beautiful vistas and explore interesting doorways. There are many lovely turn-of-the-century and art-deco buildings and small pocket-parks. Public art abounds, thanks to the "One Percent for Art" program which designates 1% of certain City Capital Improvement Program funds for artworks. The two most notable works are the **Alexander Calder mobile** currently at the Fourth and Blanchard Building and **Henry Moore's *Three Piece Vertebrae*** at the 1001 Building on Fourth Avenue. Free maps of the downtown area are available from concierges at most hotels and at the Visitor Information Center at the corner of Seventh Avenue and Stewart Street operated by the Seattle/King County Convention and Visitors Bureau. Note: Seattle police enforce the no-jaywalking law; a ticket for **jaywalking** costs $19.

Metered parking is available on the streets; no-parking hours depend upon locations. Most of the parking lots are privately owned and rates may vary widely; check around a little before parking. Currently, most lots charge between $3-$5 for two hours. Try parking by the Kingdome on the south or by Seattle Center to the north and taking public transportation around downtown.

Metro

Metro buses are free from 4am to 9pm in the downtown **Free Bus Zone** (also known as the **Magic Carpet**) which extends from First Avenue to Sixth Avenue/or the I-5 Freeway between Jackson on the south and Bell on the north. It makes taking a walking tour of the city easy—just hop on a free bus when you're tired. Most bus stops have route maps and schedules for the buses using that stop and schedules are available in many downtown banks, hotels, offices and the Seattle Public Library. Several types of passes are available; on Saturdays and Sundays a $1 all-day pass may be purchased on the buses. Metro's information line operates 24 hours a day.

Cost:	One zone, $.55 non-peak; $.75 peak hours, 6am-9am & 3pm-6pm. Exact change required.
Hours:	Vary with routes.
Phone:	447-4800 for route & schedule info.

Metro's one-day Visitor Pass for sightseeing costs $2.50 and includes the Waterfront Streetcar and a round-trip ride on the Monorail. Call Metro's Customer Assistance, 447-4824, for information.

The Waterfront Streetcar

Metro's vintage Australian streetcars run along Alaskan Way on the Waterfront from Pier 70 at the north end to Yesler Way on the south, making several stops in between. A ticket is good for 1 1/2 hours, allowing passengers to get off and on while sightseeing along the waterfront. Street-cars come about every 20 minutes.

Hours:	7:15am-6:15pm daily; 7:15am-11pm, summer.
Cost:	$.55 non-peak, $.75 peak hours.
Phone:	447-4800 (Metro).

The Monorail

The Monorail, built for the 1962 World's Fair, shuttles between downtown Seattle and Seattle Center. It currently departs every 15 minutes from the Monorail platform on Fifth Avenue and Stewart Street across from the Westin Hotel (eventually, it will use the new entrance on the third floor of the Westlake Mall) and takes 90 seconds to go to its station at Center House near the Space

Needle. Or catch it at Seattle Center and ride to downtown.

Hours:	10am-9pm daily; 10am-midnight, summer.
Cost:	Adults, $.60 each way; seniors, $.25; children under 5, free.
Phone:	684-7340.

Gray Line

During the summer, Gray Line has two downtown trolley-buses that shuttle between the hotels, Seattle Center, Pioneer Square, and the waterfront. They operate between May and October and connect with Gray Line tours and the Victoria ships.

Cost:	Adults, $2 (all-day pass); children under 12, free.
Phone:	626-6088.

Taxis

Taxis are available at major destinations and hotels and may be called or flagged down. Yellow Cab and Farwest are the major companies and there are many small, independent companies. Rates vary; it may pay to compare prices.

PART I

Downtown

The Pike Place Market

The Pike Place Market has been a unique Seattle institution since it opened in 1907. Started because housewives objected to the high prices middlemen charged, it is the oldest continuously operating farmers' market in the United States. The Market includes several buildings on Pike Place, Post Alley and First Avenue between Pike and Virginia Streets. In addition to meat, fish and produce stalls, it has arts and crafts, flowers, bakeries, entertainers, small specialized restaurants, a movie theater, and shops tucked in on the

Post Alley in Pike Place Market

lower floors. It's a great place to go if you're hungry, looking for local color, looking for something unusual, looking for good views, or just looking.

After thriving during the first decades of its existence, the Market declined during the middle years of this century and was "saved" by a citizens' campaign mounted in the 1970s. **Tiles** with contributors' names on them pave the floor of the main Market building.

The **Pike Place Preservation and Development Association (PDA)** offers health and social services such as low-income housing, a senior center, child care, and counselling to area residents. Rachel, the life-sized brass piggy bank located under the Market's landmark clock, collects contributions for PDA projects.

The best way to see the Market is by walking. (It is wheelchair accessible.) Take a bus or park in nearby lots on Western Avenue or along the waterfront under the Alaskan Way Viaduct. Stairs, known as the **Pike Place Hillclimb**, connect the Market on the hill to the waterfront below. There is an elevator located a little north of the stairs in the Market but it is not easy to find; there is also an elevator on the Hillclimb side of the street by the stairs. Two restrooms are located on the lower floor of the main building.

An **Information Booth**, located on the corner of Pike Place and First Avenue near the clock, is staffed by volunteers. They have maps and information about the Market and will store packages for shoppers on a space-available basis.

For specific merchants, see listings in the phone book under "Pike Place Market" or call Market info. The Information Booth has a brochure which lists restaurants in the Market.

Hours: 9am-6pm, Mon.-Sat.;
                      11am-5pm Sun. Note:

some shops and stalls are
not open on Sundays.

Phone: 682-7453.

Pike Place Market Tours

Tours are available; reservations required.

Cost: Adults, $3.25; children,
$2.25.

Phone: 682-7453.

Rachel, the Market's life-sized piggy bank

The Waterfront

Seattle has many waterfronts, but "The Waterfront" refers to the mile and a half stretch along **Alaskan Way** between Main Street on the south end to Pier 70 at Broad Street on the north. The **Waterfront Streetcar** (page 8) serves the area, making several stops along Alaskan Way, so named because it was the jumping-off spot for Alaska gold seekers in the 1890s.

The piers, built at the turn of the century, are full of restaurants featuring fresh northwest seafood, souvenir shops packed full of treasures, and many attractions. Tour boats, the Washington State Ferries, the *Victoria Clipper*, and the BC Stena's *Princess Marguerite* and *Vancouver Island Princess* all are located along Alaskan Way.

Pier 48, at the foot of Main Street, is across the street from the south end of the Waterfront Trolley Line. It is currently shared by the **Alaska State Ferries** and the **BC Stena** ships. However, the summer of 1989 is the last season that ships going to Alaska will use this dock; beginning in 1990 they will depart from Bellingham.

Alaska Marine Highway

Phone: 1-800-642-0066.

On the south side of the Pier 48 terminal building the Port of Seattle has placed three large periscopes so visitors can have a close-up view of the container terminals. Go during working hours to see the port in action. Seattle is one of the largest container ports in the country and one of the busiest ports on the west coast due to its deep water harbor and its proximity to Asia.

BC Stena Line's *Princess Marguerite* and the *Vancouver Island Princess,* formerly owned by **B.C. Steamship Co.**, provide daily, year-round service between Seattle and Victoria from Pier 48.

See the section on Victoria, page 65, for more information.

Walking along Alaskan Way heading north, you will come to the cupola at the foot of Washington Street. A plaque marks the last resting spot of the sidewheel steamer the *Idaho*, a wayside mission hospital ship that sank in the harbor and was buried when the harbor was filled in.

The badly neglected grassy park adjacent to the cupola has a small patch of grass and a totem pole. The park, officially known as **Alaska Square**, is dedicated to "the tremendous importance of Alaska to its southern seaport, Seattle" by the Port of Seattle.

Pier 52 is headquarters for the **Washington State Ferries**. See Ferries, page 87.

Continuing northbound, on the south side of **Pier 54** is the Seattle Fire Department's waterfront station where Seattle's two venerable

The Waterfront: Alaskan Way & Washington Street

fireboats, the *Alki* and the *Chief Seattle*, are moored. It's a rare treat to catch them in action in Elliott Bay. Two vintage fire engines are on display afternoons and evenings.

Hours: 1pm-5pm, & 7pm-9pm.

Pier 54 also houses **Ye Olde Curiosity Shop**, which displays bizarre artifacts and antiques along with souvenir items for sale, and **Ivar's Restaurant**, known for its clams and photographs of early Seattle. A statue of Ivar feeding seagulls is on the sidewalk.

HARBOR TOURS:

Several harbor tour companies, located between Piers 54 and 57, offer views and narrations of Seattle's busy waterfront. All boats have enclosed seating areas for passengers wanting to stay inside and are handicapped accessible, although the ramps may be steep at low tide.

Major Marine Tours

Major Marine Tours depart from the south side of **Pier 54** and go clockwise around Elliott Bay. These trips emphasize the historical aspects of the harbor and include hot barbecued chicken with the tour. Beverages are available. Tours take about 50 minutes.

Hours   Every hour on the 1/2
                          hour from 12:30pm-
                          6:30pm, June-September.

Cost: Adults, $7.50; seniors, $6;
                          children, $5.

Phone: 783-8873.

Seattle Harbor Tours and **Tillicum Village Tours** share space between **Pier 55** and **Pier 56.**

Seattle Harbor Tours

The Harbor Tours' spacious boats cruise counter-clockwise around Elliott Bay for a one-hour fact-filled tour covering the past and present scene around the bay. Snacks and beverages are available on board.

Hours	12:15, 1:45 & 3:15pm, April-October with tours added in summer at 11am & 4:30pm.
Cost:	Adults, $6.50; teens & seniors, $6; children 5-11, $3; under 5, free.
Phone:	623-1445.

Tillicum Tours

Tillicum Tours combines a marine tour with a Northwest Indian salmon bake. Boats depart from Pier 56 and after a brief narrated tour around Elliott Bay they pass by Alki Point and cross Puget Sound to Blake Island Marine State Park. A dinner including salmon and clams is served in a cedar longhouse followed by a program of Northwest Coast Indian dances. There is time to see a movie about early Northwest Indian life, observe Indian artisans at work, visit the gift shop, or walk the island's natural forests and beaches. Totem poles made by local Indian craftsmen surround the lodge.

Tours take four hours; the boat trip is about 45 minutes each way. In the summer it is possible to take the 11:30 boat over and return later, allowing time to explore the island a little. Beverages of all types are available for purchase on the boat, but no alcoholic beverages are allowed on the island.

Hours:	6:30pm, May-October; plus 11:30am & 4:30pm tours in summer.

Cost:	Adults, $32; seniors, $28; teens, $21; children (6-12), $12; toddlers (3-5), $5.
Phone:	329-5700.

Gray Line Water Cruise Tours

The **Gray Line Water Cruise** at **Pier 57** is the longest of the water sightseeing tours, lasting two hours. The tour begins with a brief cruise around Elliott Bay, then goes out into Puget Sound and heads north, up through the locks, and docks at Fishermen's Terminal in Salmon Bay, where passengers are bused back to downtown Seattle. The reverse tour is also available. Deli-type food and beverages are available on board.

Hours:	Noon, April-October, with others added in summer. Call for schedule.
Cost:	Adults, $14.50; children (5-12), $7.50; under 5, free.
Phone:	441-1887.

The Water Link

The small Water Link maritime exhibit is located about halfway out on Pier 57, accessible from either dock level or up the ramps from the Waterfront Park. It has low-key, informative exhibits of Puget Sound's waterfronts.

Hours:	Open in the summer only; Tues.-Sun., noon-6pm.
Cost:	Adults, $1; children under 12, free.
Phone:	543-0206.

Pier 57 has several shops and restaurants – great for browsing – and public restrooms.

The benches in the brick-lined **Waterfront Park** between Pier 57 and Pier 59 are good spots to pause and take in the activity in Elliott Bay. The parade of ferries, tankers, and tugboats with their barges is spellbinding to watch. The park also has a statue of Christopher Columbus and a fountain.

For great views, walk out to the end of Piers 57 and 59. Through the coin-operated telescopes you can see West Seattle and **Alki Point** where Seattle's first settlers arrived in 1851.

The Aquarium

The Seattle Aquarium is in the center of the waterfront on **Pier 59** at the foot of the **Pike Place Hillclimb**. Exhibits focus on the Pacific marine habitat and include an outstanding coral reef, seals and playful otters, and an overhead glass-domed underwater room that surrounds viewers with northwest marine life. It also has a hands-on "touch tank," a salmon ladder and environmental information. Hint: It can be cool inside.

Food not allowed inside, none for sale; two restrooms inside the main (first) building. Gift shop adjacent; restaurant outside.

Hours:	10am-5pm, daily; 10am-7pm, summer.
Cost:	Adults, $3.25; youths (13-18) & seniors, $1.50; children (6-12), $.75; under 6, free.
Phone:	625-4357.

A restaurant, gift shop, and public restrooms are on the pier.

Omnidome

The Omnidome, also on Pier 59, is across the lobby from the Aquarium. It features glorious nature films such as "The Eruption of Mount St. Helens" on its 180° curved dome movie screen. Refreshment stand in lobby. A combination ticket for both the Omnidome and Aquarium is available.

Hours:	10am-5pm, daily; 10am-7pm, summer. Admission every 20 minutes between movies.
Cost:	Adults, $4.50; youths (13-18) & seniors, $3.50; children (6-12), $2.75; under 6, free.
Phone:	622-1868.

The two piers to the north are unoccupied, awaiting new harborfront plans.

The large gray building at **Pier 66** is the **Port of Seattle** headquarters. In addition to its extensive waterfront activities, the Port also runs Sea-Tac Airport, Fishermen's Terminal, and the pleasure boat marina at Shilshole. The last remaining fish processor on the downtown waterfront is also on Pier 66.

Next, to the north, is the **Edgewater Hotel** on Pier 67, the only hotel on the waterfront.

Pier 69 is home for the catamaran, the *Victoria Clipper,* which commutes to Victoria. See the section on Victoria, page 66, for more information.

Pier 70, at the north end of the waterfront, was built in 1901 for the large ships of the time and later was used to store canned salmon. The pier now holds several shops and restaurants with terrific views, as well as a public parking lot upstairs.

The northern terminus of the **Waterfront Streetcar** is across the street from Pier 70. **Myrtle Edwards Park** stretches 1 1/2 miles north along the waterfront.

Pioneer Square

Pioneer Square, at the south end of town, is "old Seattle" where Seattle grew and flourished in the late 1800s. The area's original wooden buildings built by Seattle's first settlers were destroyed in the **Great Seattle Fire** in 1889. To prevent another fire the city required that new buildings be built of brick. The merchants rushed to rebuild and most of the buildings were constructed in the decade before the turn of the century, giving the area an architecturally harmonious feeling.

In the years following World War I, businesses left the area and moved northward. **Skid Road**, now **Yesler Street**, which pioneers had used to slide logs down to Henry Yesler's mill, came to be synonymous with the down-and-out people who remained in the area. After several decades of neglect, Pioneer Square was rediscovered in the 1960s and 1970s and the attractive buildings have been restored for shops and offices.

The broad, tree-lined sidewalks make browsing along the shops delightful. Many art galleries, boutiques, antique shops, theaters, bookstores and restaurants are nestled in this area. There are small parks and sidewalk cafes to enjoy in good weather. Like Pike Place Market, Pioneer Square is an officially designated historical district. Brochures for self-guided walking tours are available at shops in the area.

Pioneer Square is bordered on the south by the Kingdome and the **King Street Station (Amtrak)**, and includes the area between Cherry and King Streets from the waterfront east to roughly Second or Third Avenues. The white terra cotta **Smith Tower** on the corner of Second Avenue and Jefferson, built in 1914, was for many years the tallest building west of the Mississippi. Tours of the **Chinese Throne Room** on the tower's top floor by way of one of the antique brass elevators are available; purchase tickets in the tobacco shop.

Smith Tower Tours

Hours: 9am-5pm daily; call to
                    verify.

Cost: Adults, $2; children &
                    seniors, $1.

Phone: 682-9393.

Underground Tour

The Underground Tour, an informative, light-
hearted history of Seattle and especially the
Pioneer Square area, begins with an entertaining
half-hour talk followed by a guided walking tour
of the area. The "Underground" exists because the
city raised the level of the streets several years
after the buildings were built, thereby burying the
lower floors of the buildings.

Tours start at **Doc Maynard's Public House**
across the street from the totem pole on First
Avenue between Cherry and James. Some walk-
ways and stairs have uneven surfaces; not wheelchair accessible. Food is available at Doc
Maynard's and other area restaurants before and
after tours; no restrooms on tour.

Hours: 11am, 2 & 4pm, plus
                    others added. Summer
                    (July & August): 10,
                    11am; 1, 2, 3, 4, & 6pm.
                    Call to verify.

Cost: Adults, $4; students (13-
                    17), $3.25; seniors, $2.50;
                    children (6-12), $2.75.

Phone: 682-1511.

Klondike Museum   117 South Main Street

There are some real treasures in this area. One
is the tiny Klondike Gold Rush National Park

Visitor Center, which is not a park at all but a one-room museum in a small Pioneer Square building. It is filled with historical information about the Alaska Gold Rush, set off when the steamer *Portland* landed in Seattle in 1897 with the legendary "ton of gold" from Alaska. The park rangers

Pioneer Square

have several movies available depicting the history of Seattle and its role in the Alaska Gold Rush.

Hours:	9am-5pm, daily.
Cost:	Free.
Phone:	442-7220.

Waterfall Park   Corner of 2nd Ave. & Main

Another jewel is the almost hidden Waterfall Garden built and maintained by the Annie E. Casey Foundation in honor of United Parcel Service employees. The Casey family founded the UPS company on this spot in 1907. In addition to its 22-foot man-made waterfall and lush garden plantings, it has sheltered tables and a snack bar.

Hours:	Daily, 10am-5pm; summer, 10am-7pm.

Information Booth

An information booth staffed by the Assistance League of Seattle is located on Occidental Avenue and Main Street. Open only in the summer.

Hours:	10:30am-3:00pm Tues.-Sat., June 1-September 1.

Public restrooms: on the Main Street side of the fire station at Second Avenue and Main Street.

Getting to Pioneer Square

By car: Drive south on First or Third Avenues; there are many lots near the Kingdome; prices vary. Walk north along any of the streets to Pioneer Square; there's lots to see on all of them.

By bus: take a bus heading south on First Avenue and get off near Yesler Street, by the pergolo. Call Metro, 447-4800, for information.

Or take the Waterfront Streetcar to its southern terminus and walk east to First Avenue.

The Kingdome

The Kingdome is the massive concrete mushroom-like building just south of Pioneer Square. Officially known as the **King County Stadium**, it is where the Seahawks (football) and Mariners (baseball) play their games. It also hosts trade shows, concerts and special events and can hold up to 65,000 fans depending on the event. Its self-supporting concrete roof, the world's largest, allows unobstructed views for everyone. Completed in 1976 for $63 million, it is one the few super-domes in the country to be profitable.

Tours are available, depending upon event scheduling, and may include a team practice. The souvenir shop is open during tours and events. Tours meet at Gate D and exit at Gate B.

Kingdome Tours

Hours: 3pm, winters; 11am, 1 & 3pm, summers. Call to verify.

Cost: Adults/teens, $2.50; seniors/children, $1.25.

Phone: 296-DOME.

Getting to the Kingdome

By car: Drive south on First or Third Avenues, or along Alaskan Way. Parking: There are many lots near the Kingdome; prices vary.

By bus, take a bus heading south on First Avenue. Extra buses are added for special events. Call Metro, 447-4800, for information.

Or take the Waterfront Streetcar to its southern terminus at Main Street and walk east to First Avenue.

The International District

The International District, heart of Seattle's large Asian community, covers the blocks east of the railroad tracks to the I-5 freeway and is bounded by Yesler on the north and Weller on the south. Look for the distinctive oriental street lights. The area's cultural diversity, art and architecture is best seen by walking.

The view of Elliott Bay from **Kobe Terrace Park** at the top of South Washington Street is spectacular. The park's centerpiece, the **10-ton Japanese lantern,** was given to Seattle by her sister city, Kobe, Japan. The park lies just above the **Nippon Kan Theatre** and the hillside "**Pea Patch**" gardens where neighborhood residents grow traditional fruits and vegetables.

Down the hill, Jackson Street, King Street and the side streets are lined with stores, businesses and restaurants. Note the historic tong (family association) buildings with ornate balconies and public rooms on the top floors and hotels or offices below. The historic **Chinese Bulletin Board** around the corner from King Street on Maynard Alley continues to function as a communications center for the neighborhood. **Hing Hay Park** with its red pavilion and dragon mural, the sculpture by George Tsutakawa up the street on Maynard, and the playground equipment designed by his son reflect the unique character of the neighborhood. **Uwajimaya's**, a combination department store, grocery store and restaurant, is the largest Japanese store in North America.

The **Wing Luke Museum's** exhibits trace the history of Asian groups in Seattle. In addition, it features Asian folk art, work by local artists and a gift shop.

Wing Luke Museum   407 7th Avenue So.

Hours: 11am-4:30pm Tues.-Fri.;
                noon-4pm Sat. & Sun.

Cost: Adults, $1.50; seniors and
                children, $.50.

Phone: 623-5124.

Chinatown Tours

A self-guided tour beginning with a half-hour narrated slide show in the historic Nippon Kan Theatre. Call for hours and information.

Cost: $2.00.

Phone: 624-6342.

Chinatown Discovery Tours

An extensive guided tour of the International area; tour lasts three hours and includes dim sum lunch. Reservations required.

Hours: 10:30am.

Cost: Adults, $18; seniors, $16;
                children, $12 (lunch in-
                cluded). No credit cards.

Phone: 447-9230.

Getting to the International District:

Driving: Go south on Fifth Avenue to Jackson Street; there are parking lots in the International District or near the Kingdome.

By bus: The free bus zone extends up Jackson to the freeway at 9th Avenue and includes the International District. Call Metro, 447-4800, for information.

Seattle Center

Seattle Center, the site of the 1962 World's Fair, is now an urban park with several permanent attractions, the city's cultural facilities, and attractive grounds filled with art, gardens and fountains.

Seattle's trademark, the **Space Needle**, is located on the corner of Fifth Avenue and Broad Street. Built by private citizens who wanted an eye-catching symbol for the World's Fair, the Space Needle offers one of the best views of Seattle and Puget Sound. The Observation Deck at the top (520 feet) has information about sights below and in the distance. There are two restaurants on the rotating level just below. One is more elegant (expensive) than the other, but both have the same outstanding view. The elevator ride is free for restaurant patrons. Both restaurants are very popular; to be sure of getting in, make reservations: 443-2100. There is a small cocktail lounge on the restaurant level; the elevator ride is not free for that. The 100-foot level is used for meetings and banquets. Gift and souvenir shops are on both the street and the observation levels; minimal restroom facilities.

The Space Needle Observation Deck

The elevator ride to the observation deck at the top of the needle takes approximately 90 seconds.

Hours: 8am-midnight (varies with
                 seasons & weekends).

Cost: Adults, $3.75; 5-12,
                 $2.00; under 5, free.

Phone: 443-2100.

Monorail

The Monorail terminal is across from the Space Needle entrance to the north. Built to carry people to the 1962 World's Fair, the Monorail shuttles between the downtown station at Fifth Avenue and Stewart Street and Seattle Center every 10-15 minutes.

Cost: Adults, $.60; seniors, $.25, each way. children under 5, free.

Information

The **Visitors' Information Booth**, staffed by the knowledgeable people of the Seattle/King County Convention and Visitors' Bureau, is across from the Monorail ramp next to the Gray Line booth.

Hours: 10am-6pm daily from Memorial Day to Labor Day.

Phone: 447-4244.

There are also two information booths in Center House. Maps of the Seattle Center grounds are available at the booths.

Center House

As you walk west from either the Monorail or the Space Needle, the next major building is Center House. Built as armory in 1939, it is a large gray-green building which, desspite valiant remodeling efforts, retains its utilitarian appearance. (Note the art deco eagles over the lower back doorway on the stadium side.) Used as the **Food Circus** during the World's Fair, it houses food and gift shops. The restaurants are primarily ethnic fast-food places; a few serve alcoholic beverages. It's a good place to go when everyone wants something different. Gift shops are on the top and lower floors. Often there are exhibits or entertainment. Center House houses two information booths, one near the Monorail entrance and the other in the back; a cash machine (Accel) at the top of the escalator; executive offices for Seattle Center, the Seattle Symphony, and the Seattle Opera; meeting rooms; police and security; and there are **restrooms** on all three floors toward the back (north). (There are also restrooms on the grounds under the Flag Pavilion and on the corner of the NW Court Buildings near the Coliseum.)

Restaurant & shop hours:	11am-7pm or later; call for info. Breakfast places open earlier.

Seattle Center information:

Phone:	684-7165 (recording) or 684-7200.

The Children's Museum

The Children's Museum is located on the lower level of Center House, at the foot of the stairs by the fountain. It has a small neighborhood for children to play in as well as many wonderful hands-on exhibits and changing shows.

Hours:	10am-5pm, Tues.-Sun. Closed Mon.
Cost:	$2.50 per person; children under 12 months, free.
Phone:	441-1767.

The **Seattle Center House Theater** is adjacent to the Children's Museum on the lower level. It houses the **Piccoli Children's Theatre**. Performances are Tuesdays-Sundays during the summer and Thursdays-Sundays the rest of the year.

Piccoli Children's Theatre

Phone:	441-5080.

The Group Theater

The Group Theater also holds its performances in the Center House Theater, Tuesdays-Sundays.

Phone: 543-4237.

The Fun Forest

The Fun Forest, as the amusement park is known, covers the grounds between Center House and the Space Needle. The rides are divided into two sections, one for younger and one for older kids. There are also games, miniature golf, a video arcade, and refreshment and souvenir stands. Prices of rides and games vary.

Hours: Summer: daily, noon-midnight; spring & fall: most weekends, depending upon the weather.

Phone: 684-7200 or 684-7165 (recording).

In the summer, concerts are held two or three times a week on the **Mural Amphitheatre** stage. The Venetian glass tile mosiac wall was designed by Paul Horiuchi for the World's Fair.

The Pacific Science Center

The Pacific Science Center is a legacy of the World Fair's U.S. Science Pavilion. It has marvellous hands-on exhibits for all ages, an Indian longhouse, scientific exhibits, a **Planetarium**, a building for special exhibits, a **Laserium**, and the 3-story **IMAX movie theater**. The gift shop and the deli-type restaurant are open to the public without an admission fee. There are several restrooms in the Science Center buildings.

The Science Center is located on the Second Avenue side of Seattle Center; from the Space Needle or Center House, pass by the Mural

Amphitheater and look for the Science Center's graceful white arches.

Hours: 10am-5pm weekdays;
                    10am-6pm weekends;
                    10am-9pm Thurs.
                    Summer: 10am-6pm
                    daily, 10am-9pm Thurs.

Cost: Adults, $4.00; juniors &
                    seniors, $3.00; 2-5, $2.00
                    (admission prices for ex-
                    hibits only). The Laserium
                    and IMAX theaters have
                    additional fees.

Phone: 443-2001 or 443-2880
                    (recording).

Pacific Arts Center

The Pacific Arts Center has children's art classes and exhibits, and an auditorium used for plays and special exhibits.

Phone: 443-5437.

The **Flag Pavilion** houses special functions and exhibits. The **Flag Plaza** in front of it is often the site of concerts.

The **Coliseum**, near the International Fountain, is home for the Seattle SuperSonics basketball games and is also used for special events.

Northwest Crafts Center

The Northwest Crafts Center exhibits and sells fine examples of Northwest pottery and other craft items. It is located in the low building on the north side of the Coliseum facing the International Fountain.

Hours: 11am-6pm Tues.-Sun.;
                    Summer: 11am-6pm daily.

Cost: Free.

Phone: 728-1555.

The **International Fountain** in front of the
Coliseum is another relic from the World's Fair.
Fashioned to look like an abstract sunflower (not
a hand grenade, as a local writer has suggested),
the fountain is beautiful when the water is spray-
ing and the music is playing.

The buildings (the **Bagley Wright Theatre,
Playhouse**, and **Opera House**) along Mercer
Street house Seattle's performing arts: the symphony, ballet, opera, and theater companies. They
are generally open only for performances. However, the Bagley Wright has public tours, by ap-
pointment only, phone 443-2210. Exhibits and
trade shows are held in the **Exhibition Hall**; the
Arena is a multi-purpose building used for ice
hockey, trade shows, banquets, etc.

On a nice day, a stroll around Seattle Center's
74-acre landscaped grounds with its many small
courtyards, fountains and artworks is delightful.

Getting to Seattle Center:

In addition to the Monorail, page 28, several
buses go to Seattle Center. #3, 4, 6, & 16 stop on
the Space Needle side on 5th Avenue; #1, 2, 13,
15, & 18 stop on 1st Avenue North by the
Coliseum. Call Metro, 447-4800, for information.

Or take the Waterfront Streetcar to its northern
terminus at Broad Street and walk five blocks up
Broad Street to Seattle Center.

Driving: There are many parking lots nearby;
prices vary. Valet parking is offered by the Space
Needle for restaurant patrons.

In and Around

The Locks

The **Hiram M. Chittenden Locks**, known variously as the **Chittenden Locks**, the **Government Locks**, the **Salmon Ladder**, or simply the **Locks**, are located on the west end of the Lake Washington Ship Canal, which is also known as the Ship Canal. Completed in 1916, the locks are used by pleasure boaters and commercial ships going between saltwater Puget Sound and freshwater Lake Union and Lake Washington. The present Salmon Ladder was built in 1976 to facilitate the salmon's migration back to their freshwater spawning grounds.

Although visiting the locks is always popular, it's especially nice to do on a sunny summer day. There are always boats going through the locks and the hustle and bustle of the boats' crews and lock operators is fun to watch. Visitors may walk across the locks while the lock gates are closed. The Salmon Ladder with underwater windows for viewing the salmon is on the south side of the locks. The heaviest salmon runs are in November, January, and the summer months, but there are always some fish. In recent years sea lions have been visible on the west side of the locks as they graze on the salmon returning to their spawning grounds. The beautifully landscaped **Carl S. English, Jr. Ornamental Gardens** on the terraces of the north side and **Commodore Park** on the south are perfect for taking in the action or relaxing with a picnic lunch.

The Visitor Center, located on the north side, has interesting displays and a narrated slide show about the locks. Restrooms are located on both the north and south sides. A cart selling snacks and hot dogs is usually by the north entrance, and several restaurants are nearby on the north side.

To learn more about the locks and salmon ladder, take the guided walking tour.

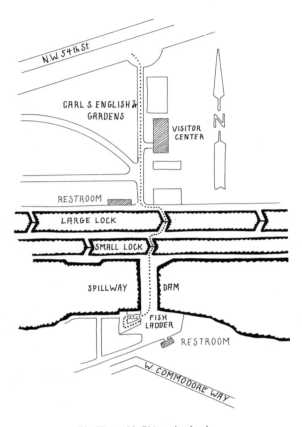

The Hiram M. Chittenden Locks

Tours: June 15-September 15,
                daily at 2pm & 3:30pm;
                September 15-June 15,
                Sat. & Sun. at 2pm, at the
                Visitor Center.

Cost: Free.

Hours:	The locks and salmon ladder are always open to boats and fish, but the Visitor Center and park grounds open at 7am and close around dusk; the Visitor Center is closed Tues. & Wed. in winter.
Cost:	Free.
Phone:	783-7059.

Getting to the Locks:

Driving: From downtown Seattle, take Westlake Avenue to the Fremont Bridge and bear left onto Fremont Avenue at the second light from the north end of the bridge. (Richard Beyer's popular sculpture *"Waiting for the Interurban"* is on the right side at the north end of the Fremont Bridge.) Continue bearing left on Leary Way into Ballard and turn left onto Market Street; the locks are approximately a mile farther to the west on the left side of the street.

Or, go north on Elliott Avenue across the Ballard Bridge to the exit at the north end of the bridge; turn left, go under the bridge and continue bearing left, following the signs, to Market Street; turn left (west) onto Market Street in Ballard to the Locks on the lefthand side of the road.

From downtown Seattle, the drive will take approximately 15-20 minutes.

By bus: Take bus #17 from downtown. Call Metro, 447-4800, for information.

Gray Line's City Bus Tours usually stop on the south side of the Locks. Call Gray Line, 626-5208.

Daybreak Star Indian Cultural Center

Located in the northwest corner of **Discovery Park**, which was formerly **Fort Lawton**, the Cultural Center features artwork done by Native Americans. The building has several large pieces of art, a small gallery which shows works by contemporary artists, and a gift shop with attractive items, books and cards. The Center also has community center facilities, including meeting rooms, day care and outdoor playground equipment.

Hours:	10am-5pm, Wed.-Sun.
Cost:	Free.
Phone:	285-4425.

The grounds have more works of art, including one of the large terra cotta Indians saved from the White Henry Stuart building when it was demolished. The view looking north to Shilshole Marina and up Puget Sound to Whidbey Island and beyond is one of the most spectacular in Seattle.

Getting to Daybreak Star

By car: Follow Commodore Way from the south side of the locks heading west into Discovery Park and take the first right turn.

By bus: Metro bus #33 from downtown Seattle goes to Discovery Park and Daybreak Star Cultural Center. Call Metro, 447-4800, for information.

Fishermen's Terminal

Fishermen's Terminal at **Salmon Bay,** one of Seattle's busy working waterfronts, is home of one of the world's largest fleet of salmon and halibut trollers. The facilities have been renovated recently, with buildings and docks enlarged to accommodate modern fishing boats and processors.

Signs of the fishing industry abound: nets dry on the pavement and in the oversized sheds at the east end of the buildings, boats of all types line the wharves, and marine hardware supplies are available at several chandleries. **Chinook's** restaurant's walls are covered with pictures of local boats and crews and the Terminal's restaurants and bars cater to the fishermen and visitors. On warm days there is outside service.

There are benches near the **Seattle Fishermen's Memorial statue** to rest on while taking in the scene. Fish engravings on the glass bricks in the Terminal Center building represent local species.

The shops in the Terminal stock gear and supplies for the fishing fleet. **Captain's** has navigation charts, an extensive collection of books about boats and fishing, and some nautical gifts, including globes. A pipe and tobacco shop is planned. Public restrooms and telephones are near the **Bay Cafe**.

For information, phone 728-3395.

Getting to Fishermen's Terminal:

From downtown Seattle, head north on Elliott Avenue, bearing right as it becomes 15th Avenue West. Continue heading north to the Emerson Street exit. Watch for signs for Fishermen's Terminal, just south of the Ballard Bridge.

By bus: Take bus #15 or 18 from downtown Seattle. Call Metro, 447-4800, for information.

Woodland Park Zoo

Seattle's Woodland Park Zoo has won recognition and awards in recent years for its new natural exhibits, the African Savanna, the Australasia exhibit, the Wetlands area, and its most recent addition, the Asian Forest for elephants. The Nocturnal House is full of large-eyed, rarely seen animals. The immaculate grounds are beautifully landscaped and have helpful, informative signs. A feeling of respect for animals and the environment pervades the exhibits.

There is a Family Farm area with typical farm animals and, depending on the season, their babies. This area has the "Animal Contact Area" which is commonly referred to as the Petting Zoo. A viewing mound in the African Savanna area has a brass plaque in memory of rock star **Jimi Hendrix.** A bald eagle, several recovering eagles, and a Northwest Environment exhibit are tucked away by the West Entrance.

There is a large grassy area for picnics and there are many tables on the grounds. Refreshment stands and restrooms are scattered throughout the zoo.

Strollers and wheelchairs may be rented, depending upon availability, at the ARC building, inside the West Entrance on the left.

Hours: Daily, April-September, 8:30am-6pm; March & October, 8:30am-5pm; November-February, 8:30am-4pm. Note: Some exhibits and refreshment stands close early.

Cost: Adults, $3.50; youths (6-17), seniors, & disabled, $1.75; children under 6, free. Reduced prices November-February.

Phone:	684-4800, or 789-7919 (recording).

Getting to the Zoo:

Driving: From downtown Seattle, take I-5 heading north to exit #169, 50th Street, and head west, following the signs. There are also signs from the 45th Street exit from I-5.

Or, from Hwy 99, head north and exit at 45th Avenue. Turn left at the stop sign onto 45th Avenue and head west, staying in the right-hand lane, to Fremont Avenue. Turn right onto Fremont Avenue and go north to 50th Avenue to the South Entrance of the Zoo. There are pay parking lots near the entrances on 50th and Fremont Avenue, the West Entrance on Phinney Avenue, and the North Entrance on 59th Street.

By bus: Take bus #5 from downtown Seattle directly to the West Entrance. Call Metro, 447-4800, for information.

Woodland Park Rose Garden

The formal Rose Garden on the south side of the Zoo is open the same hours as the Zoo.

Cost:	Free.
Phone:	684-4075.

The Zoo occupies the west half of **Woodland Park**; **Green Lake** is to the north.

The University of Washington

The University of Washington, the premiere school in the state university system, is a few minutes north of downtown, just east of the I-5 freeway. Theaters, museums, libraries, athletic facilities and classroom buildings for the university's 35,000 students are located throughout the spacious grounds.

The Olmsted brothers, planners of New York's Central Park and Seattle's extensive park system, designed the campus for Seattle's 1909 Alaskan-Yukon Exposition. The **Drumheller Fountain** in the middle of **Frosh Pond** and the breathtaking view of Mt. Rainier continue to be the campus's centerpiece. There are many gardens and groves throughout the grounds; one of the most interesting is the **Medicinal Herb (or Drug Plant) garden** across from the Forestry buildings.

The university's two major museums are open to the public. The **Burke Museum** (phone 543-5590) at the north end of the campus has permanent early Northwest Native American and natural history exhibits on the lower floor and changing shows on the main floor. A side room on the main floor dedicated to the Burke family has stunning Tiffany glass windows and the coffee shop downstairs is in an elegant room with panelling from an 18th-century European chateau. The **Henry Art Gallery** (phone 543-2280), on 15th Avenue across from Campus Parkway, holds changing fine art exhibits.

The school has spread beyond the original grounds to include buildings scattered throughout the 694-acre campus. **Husky Stadium** and **Hec Edmundson Pavilion**, where the UW's Husky teams play, are on the campus's east side along Montlake Boulevard. The unusual man-made **climbing rock** is in the parking lot near the Water

Activities Building. The medical complex is on NE Pacific Street along the Montlake Cut (or Canal) on the south side.

Campus maps and information are available at **Schmitz Hall**, room 320, at 15th Avenue and Campus Parkway and at the booths at campus entrances. To drive through the campus, ask for a free 15-minute pass at a ticket booth. Parking is available in campus lots.

Free **guided campus tours** lasting approximately 1 1/2 hours are given 2:30pm weekdays, departing from Schmitz Hall, room 320. Phone 543-9686 for information.

The Visitor Information Center, 4014 University Way NE, has information and a Campus Walk map.

Hours: 8am-5pm weekdays.

Phone: 543-9198.

Getting to the University:

By car: Take I-5 heading north to the 45th Street exit. Head east on 45th Street, following the signs, to the northern campus entrance on the right at 17th Avenue.

By bus: Several buses, #70, 71, 72, 73, 74, & 83, go to the the university area. Because the campus is so large, call Metro, 447-4800, for information to go to a specific area.

The Arboretum

The Washington Park Arboretum, the large, quiet, city park between Madison Avenue and Lake Washington, is part of Seattle's extensive park system designed by the Olmsted brothers, the team famous for designing New York's Central Park. Plantings are grouped by species with informative signs. The rhododendrons, Washington's state flower, and azaleas are spectacular in the spring when they are in bloom. It's a nice place to visit on foot or bicycle for a picnic lunch. In the summer, swimmers and canoeists enjoy the water around **Foster Island** at the north end of the park. A trail through Foster Island begins at the **Museum of History and Industry** and is accessible from the land north of the Arboretum.

Lake Washington Boulevard meanders through the Arboretum from Madison Avenue to the University, but Arboretum Drive East, the high road to the east, is more scenic and slower paced. The Arboretum and Arboretum Drive East close at sunset but the main roads remain open all the time.

Hours:	Open daily 8am - sunset.
Cost:	Free.
Phone:	543-8800.

The Visitor Information Center

The Visitor Information Center is located in the northeast section, on Arboretum Drive East. Its shop sells books, plant accessories and a small selection of plants. Restrooms are located in the building.

Hours:	10am-4pm weekdays; 12noon-4pm weekends.

| Tours: | Free guided walking tours depart from the Visitor Information Center Sundays at 1pm. |

Japanese Garden

An authentic Japanese Garden covering 3 1/2 acres is located in the southwest corner of the Arboretum grounds. The garden has been described as "a compressed world of mountains, forest, lakes, rivers, tablelands, and a village, each with a quiet message of its own." A **Japanese Tea Service** is performed the third Sunday of the month. Note: The gravel pathways may be difficult for wheelchairs and strollers to negotiate.

| Hours: | 10am-4pm weekdays; noon-4pm weekends, March-November. |

| Cost: | Adults, $1.50; 19 & under and seniors, $.75; under 6, free. |

| Phone: | 684-4725. |

Getting to the Arboretum:

By car: To the Arboretum's north end: From downtown Seattle, take I-5 heading north. Take exit #168B (Bellevue-Kirkland) to Hwy 520. Stay in the right lane and take the first exit, approximately one mile (Montlake/University of Washington). Stay in the right lane of the exit ramp and go straight through the intersection; the road becomes Lake Washington Boulevard. Bear left after approximately 1/2 mile when the road forks at 24th Avenue. At the stop sign in the middle of the intersection, go left to the Information Center and Arboretum Drive East (the sign says "Office & Greenhouse") or right along Lake Washington Boulevard.

Or, to the south end: Drive east on Madison Avenue to Lake Washington Boulevard and the entrance to the Arboretum is on the left.

By bus: Take #11 to the southern Arboretum entrance at the intersection of Madison Avenue and Lake Washington Boulevard. The Japanese Garden is about a quarter mile to the north; the Visitor Center approximately one mile.

Or take #43 or #48 to the northern end at 24th Avenue and East Lynn. The Visitor Center is approximately 1/4 mile to the east.

The Washington Park Arboretum

Museum of Flight

The Museum of Flight, Seattle's newest museum, has two outstanding galleries filled with facts and flying machines. Visits start with planes on the grounds outside the museum. Inside, in the restored Red Barn where Boeing built its first planes, there are informative exhibits depicting the history of flight. Planes hang from the ceiling and are displayed on the floor of the elegant glass-walled Great Gallery. The view from the mezzanine balcony is superb.

Museum docents are available for short introductory tours, more extensive tours, or just to answer visitors' questions. Films about man and flight are shown daily in the theater, and special programs and films are scheduled throughout the year. A gift shop is located off the entry lobby. Currently there is no food service, but a restaurant is planned for 1989. Restrooms are on the east side of the Great Gallery.

The museum is located on the west side of Boeing Field, also known as the King County Airport, about 15 minutes from downtown Seattle. The address is 9404 E. Marginal Way South.

Hours: 10am-5pm daily;
                Thurs., 10am-9pm.

Price: Adults, $4.00; 13-18,
                $3.00; 6-12, $2.00; under
                6, free.

Phone: 764-5720.

Getting to the Museum of Flight:

Driving: From downtown Seattle, take I-5 heading south to exit #158 at the south end of Boeing Field. Head west for half a mile, then turn right onto E. Marginal Way South and head north. The parking entrance is on the south side of the Red Barn.

Or take Hwy 99 heading south, keeping to the left when the road forks at the First Avenue South bridge; the road becomes East Marginal Way South. The entrance to the museum is on the left, just after the Red Barn.

By bus: Bus #174. Call Metro, 447-4800, for information.

Out and About

Boeing Tour Center, Everett

Boeing's Everett facility is where 17,000 of Boeing's 90,000 Seattle area employees produce its wide-body planes, the 747 and 767.

Tours begin in the auditorium with an informative slide show. Visitors are then bused to the largest, by volume, building in the world to see the production line and around the grounds to see the finished products. The tour guides are knowledgeable and full of superlatives: the biggest, the most, the first, etc.

There is very little walking on the tour and it is wheelchair accessible. Children under 10 are not permitted; cameras are. The Tour Center has historical photographs, a small gift shop and restrooms.

Cost:	Free.
Hours:	Change seasonally; call to verify. Tours are weekdays only on a first-come, first- served basis.
Phone:	1-342-4801.

Getting to the Boeing Tour Center:

Driving: Go north on I-5 or on I-405 to I-5 exit #189 (approximately a half hour from Seattle). Head west (the left lane of the exit ramp) on SR 526 for three miles and follow the signs for Boeing Tour Center.

It is possible to get there by public transportation, but not easy. Start early in the morning (before 8am) and take Metro bus #6 from downtown Seattle to Aurora Avenue by Aurora Village and transfer to Community Transit bus #750. Take Community Transit to downtown Everett and transfer to Everett bus #2 at Beverly

Lane and Hewitt Avenue. Transportation time each way is approximately two hours. Phone 1-800-652-1375 for Community Transit information.

Gray Line offers Boeing tours weekday mornings from May-September with an afternoon tour added in the summer.

Cost: $16.00

Phone: 626-5208.

There are two towns not far from Everett that are interesting side trips.

Snohomish

Snohomish, located a few miles east of Everett on Rte 2, is known for its antique shops. Most are located on the main street or in the Antique Mall. The residential area on the hill has many fine turn-of-the-century Victorian homes.

Edmonds

Half-way between Seattle and Everett, a few minutes' drive to the west from I-5, is the small, attractive town of Edmonds. All roads into town lead to the ferry terminal, where the ferries to and from **Kingston** dock. South of the dock are marinas and waterfront restaurants with views of Puget Sound and Kitsap Peninsula. Fifth Avenue, the main street heading toward the water, is lined with flowers, small shops, galleries and restaurants. The **Old Milltown** shopping center and a log cabin housing the Chamber of Commerce office (phone 1-776-6711) are on the south side of Fifth Avenue North as it comes into town.

Getting to Edmonds

Look for the Edmonds/Kingston Ferry signs on I-5 and follow the road into town; however, stay alert as you approach downtown to avoid getting into the ferry-traffic lane.

Snoqualmie Falls

Spectacular Snoqualmie Falls is located just outside of the small town of Snoqualmie, an easy 45-minute drive from Seattle. Most people visit during the summer months, but to appreciate the majesty of the 268-foot falls, go after heavy rains or during spring run-offs. An observation deck and covered picnic tables are nearby, as well as a snack bar, souvenir shop and restrooms. A trail from the top leads down to the old Puget Power plant at the base of the falls.

The **Salish Lodge** overlooking the falls features huge, elegant brunches daily; call ahead for reservations. The lodge's recent expansion added overnight accommodations, a country clothing shop and a lounge upstairs.

Phone: 1-888-2556.

On weekends during the summer and holidays the **Puget Sound & Snoqualmie Valley Railroad** steam train runs between North Bend and the west side of Snoqualmie Falls, with a stop in Snoqualmie. Call 1-888-3030 for information. (See Steam Trains, page 120.)

The historic **train depot** in Snoqualmie houses a small museum full of logging items from the area; the former waiting room has been turned into a bookstore. It is open on weekends when the steam train operates.

Getting to Snoqualmie Falls:

From I-90 heading east, take the Snoqualmie exit, # 27. Turn left, under the freeway, and follow the signs to Snoqualmie and Snoqualmie Falls. Turn left after 1/4 mile; go approximately 3/4 miles then left again at the stop sign, and the falls are about 3/4 mile away. The road is well-marked. Driving time from Seattle: approximately 45 minutes.

There are several places along I-90 to stop en route to the falls: **Gilman Village** in Issaquah, exit 15, has restaurants, bakeries and shops. (See Shopping, page 114.) **Boehm's Chocolates** is just east of exit 17, east of Front Street on Gilman Blvd. On clear days Mt. Rainier is visible behind the **Issaquah Alps**. The **Herbfarm**, a ten-minute drive from the Preston/Fall City exit, #22, has several gardens full of herbs; phone: 784-2222. To see the full array of plantings and the llamas and other animals, visit in spring or summer. (See Gardens, page 102). The **Snoqualmie Winery**, located on a hillside overlooking the Snoqualmie Valley, is a few miles farther east at exit 31 just off the Snoqualmie Falls exit. (See Wineries, page 129.) The **Snoqualmie Valley Historical Museum** in nearby North Bend has articles and photographs depicting life in the area from its earliest settlements.

Buses # 210, 211, 212, & 213 serve this area. Call Metro, 447-4800, for info.

Snoqualmie Falls

Mt. Rainier

When majestic Mt. Rainier is visible on the southeast horizon, Seattleites remark that "the mountain is out." At 14,411 feet, Rainier is the fifth highest mountain in the United States and the highest of the volcanic peaks in Washington.

The native Indians called it Tahoma, meaning "white mountain." In 1792 when Captain George Vancouver explored the Puget Sound region he named the mountain in honor of Peter Rainier, a fellow English sea captain.

Mt. Rainier can be seen from spots throughout the Puget Sound area (see Views, page 123), but to really appreciate its grandeur, take one of the scenic drives for a closer view.

There are several routes from Seattle to Mt. Rainier, all with spectacular views. Driving time from Seattle is approximately 2 1/2 hours each way depending upon stops. For maximum viewing, do the trip in a loop, going one way and returning another. Look for pullout spots along the road, a sign that there's something extraordinary to see—it's almost impossible to stop at every one. The side roads in the towns along the way often have fine old buildings and homes, built when the area prospered from coal, lumber or agriculture.

The highest elevation in Mt. Rainier National Park accessible by automobile is **Sunrise**, at 6,400 feet. The Visitor Information Center there has food service, campers' supplies and a gift shop. The road to Sunrise branches off from the **White River entrance** and is not open in the winter.

The facilities at **Paradise**, altitude 5,400 feet, are more extensive. There are displays and movies about the park in the large, round Visitors Center, and Park Service personnel are available to answer questions. A snack bar and gift shop are located in the Visitors Center and also in the grand old **Paradise Inn** a little farther up the road.

The Paradise Inn also has hotel facilities and a
dining room. **Note:** In the winter the Paradise Inn
is closed and the Visitors Center is open only on
weekends; however, bathroom facilities in the
Visitors Center are always open.

Trails in Rainier's sub-alpine area, marked
with approximate walking times, start from the
parking lot. Pets must be kept on leash and are not
allowed on trails.

Park admission is $5 a car.

Getting to Mt. Rainier

Through **Maple Valley** and **Enumclaw:**
Note: this entrance to Mt. Rainier is closed in
the winter.

Head east on I-90, then south on I-405 to exit
#4, marked Renton/Enumclaw SR169, south of
I-90. This exit is a little tricky; watch for the signs
to Enumclaw. Follow the road through **Maple
Valley** to **Black Diamond**, a former coal mining
area now known for its brick-oven bakery a few
blocks west of the highway. Just south of Black
Diamond the road crosses over the spectacular
Green River Gorge. There are several spots between Black Diamond and **Enumclaw** where Mt.
Rainier suddenly appears, and some side roads
around Enumclaw have wonderful views. From
Enumclaw it is approximately 40 miles to the
White River entrance on SR 410. There is a Forest
Service Information Center on the right side of the
road past Greenwater and another information center at the park entrance. **Crystal Mountain**, the
state's largest ski area, also has summer tourist
facilities; the road to Crystal is on the left just outside the gateway marking the park entrance.

Through **Puyallup** and **Longmire:**
The road from Longmire to Paradise is open
year-round, but driving restrictions may apply in
the winter (November-May). For highway information call: 1-569-2343.

Head south on I-5 to exit #142A to Puyallup
and Mt. Rainier. Follow the signs for Puyallup

(home of the Western Washington State Fair);
there isn't much warning before exits or turns.
Then follow SR 161 to Eatonville, Rte 7 to Elbe,
then Rte 706 to Ashford. Longmire is about five
miles inside of the park entrance, 95 miles
southeast of Seattle. Note: returning to Seattle,
highway signs are sparse; stay on the main road
through Puyallup until you come to signs for I-5.

Northwest Trek

Northwest Trek, a 600-acre wildlife park with
guided tours by tram, is about a half-hour south of
Puyallup.

Hours:	Summer, 9:30am-6pm daily, tours on the hour; winter, Fri.-Sun. & holidays, 9:30am-3pm.
Cost:	Adults, $5.75; seniors, $5.25; youths, 5-17, $3.50; tots, $1.50.
Phone:	1-832-6116.

The vintage **steam train** in the small town of
Elbe runs on weekends during the summer and
holidays. For information, phone the **Mt. Rainier
Scenic Railroad**, 1-569-2588.

Moore's Mountain Village with its eye-catching merry-go-round, is a little farther on. The
complex contains a restaurant, art gallery, pottery
studio and several shops.

There are several restaurants along the way
featuring homemade breads, soups and/or pies;
the **Copper Creek** restaurant in Ashford claims to
be internationally known for its homemade wild
blackberry pies.

The old **National Park Inn** at Longmire, also
known as the **Longmire Inn**, is open year-round,
8am-5pm. It has rooms, food service, souvenirs,
and some groceries; phone 1-569-2411. The
Longmire Museum next door is one of the

original Park Service Museums with exhibits describing the geology and wildlife of the park. In winter, cross-country ski equipment and information are available at the **Ski Touring Center** to the right of the Inn; phone 1-569-2412 for info.

During the winter, hours and days of operation change; call places to confirm before making plans.

For information about Mt. Rainier:

National Park Service, Tahoma Woods, Star Route, Ashford, WA, 98304. Phone: 1-569-2211.

Mt. Rainier Guest Services, P.O. Box 108, Ashford, WA, 98304. Phone: 1-569-2275.

Twenty-four hour recorded highway and general information: 1-569-2343.

The Olympic Peninsula

Travelling to the Olympic Peninsula is popular with both visitors and residents, especially in the summer. With many choices of things to do and see on the Peninsula, an itinerary depends upon the traveller's interests and schedule. Visitor Information Centers in Seattle have some information about the Olympic Peninsula but each of the major cities on the Peninsula has a Chamber of Commerce office or a Visitor Information Office with helpful brochures and staff. Offices are listed at the end of this section.

The most popular jumping-off spot for the Peninsula is the Seattle-Winslow ferry. Driving time from Winslow northwest to either Port Townsend or Port Angeles is approximately three hours but it may be longer depending upon the number of logging trucks, campers and road repairs on the two-lane highway. To appreciate the charm of the Peninsula, take side trips off the highway on the backroads. The following are some suggestions for sights to see on the west side of Puget Sound.

The jumbo ferries making the crossing between Seattle and Winslow are the largest and newest of the state ferry system. The ride over takes about half an hour and on a clear day the views are spectacular. Foot passengers can easily visit the attractive town of Winslow, a short walk from the ferry dock, and have a meal before returning to Seattle. Also, the **Bainbridge Island Winery** is within walking distance of the ferry terminal: continue straight ahead on Hwy 305 for 1/4 mile. It's open afternoons, Wednesday-Sunday.

A few miles west of the Agate Pass Bridge three striking totem poles call attention to the Indian heritage of the area. The **grave of Chief Sealth** is in Suquamish, a short distance from the totem poles. The **Suquamish Indian Museum**, about 15 minutes by car from the ferry dock, is on the left just beyond the Agate Pass bridge. This small, attractive museum has pictorial exhibits and artifacts depicting Indian life in the area.

As you continue driving northwest on Rte 305 you come next to the town of **Poulsbo**. Turn left at the first traffic light onto Hostmark Street to drive into town and the waterfront where the town's Scandinavian heritage is evident. Note: On the right on a sharp hill is a large church. Its striking Scandinavian style is now almost obscured by a new wing. It is pleasant to stroll along the waterfront park and browse in the shops and the irresistible bakery along Front Street.

Continuing northward, the road forks. To the east is **Port Gamble**, a quaint New England-style town complete with a country store and museum, but no restaurants. The ferry from Edmonds, an attractive town with flowers, shops and restaurants, leaves from **Kingston**, eight miles southeast of Port Gamble.

Or, continuing on to the Olympic Peninsula, the highway crosses the **Hood Canal Floating Bridge**, famous for sinking during a wild winter storm in 1979. The road to Port Ludlow branches off to the north just west of the Hood Canal Floating Bridge. The Resort at **Port Ludlow** is known for its tournament golf course, hotel, and marine facilities. Several roads lead to the picturesque town of **Port Townsend** which has many charming 19th-century Victorian buildings housing restaurants, shops, and bed and breakfast inns. The **Jefferson County Historical Museum** in City Hall on Water Street has photographs and articles from the times when Port Townsend was vying to become the premiere city in the Northwest. Pictorial maps for city walking tours are available at the Chamber of Commerce office on Sims Way. The dock for the Port Townsend-Keystone ferry is on the main street; the passenger-only ferry to Friday Harbor leaves from the marina at the north end of town. See Ferries, page 99.

Continuing northwest on Hwy 101 the next town is **Sequim**. To see the picturesque side that makes people want to retire here (besides the scant annual 20 inch rainfall) take the Sequim-Dungeness Road marked by signs to the 3 Crabs Restaurant. The drive includes views of **Dungeness Spit**, the **Olympic Game Farm**, pastures and tree farms.

Back on Hwy 101, the last large town on the north end of the Peninsula is **Port Angeles**. The ferry dock for the Black Ball ferry to Victoria is downtown near the Visitor Information Center. The windy walk out on **Ediz Spit** is a good way to pass the wait for the ferry. **Hurricane Ridge**, elevation 5,200 feet, is 17 miles outside town. The views along the way are spectacular, as is **Mt. Olympus** on a clear day. A fee of $3 per car is charged in the summer to enter **Olympic National Park** and the other parks on the Peninsula.

Hwy 112 splits off a few miles west of Port Angeles and stays close to the coast. The small towns along the way have supplies for the many people who come for the area's fishing. Staying on Hwy 101 to the south is **Lake Crescent**, which has lodging facilities and many hiking trails.

Hwy 101 continues on the west side of Olympic National Park passing through small towns and Indian reservations where people continue to earn their living by logging and fishing. There are few roads in the area but the hiking trails and campgrounds offer opportunities to see the natural wilderness of the area. The road is on the wet west side of the **Rain Forest** where the rainfall averages more than 150 inches a year.

Turning east at **Grays Harbor** the traveller can return to I-5 or head north on Hwy 101 and go northwest on Rte 3 to Bremerton, where the **U.S. Navy shipyards** are. The shipyard is not open to the public, but to get a good view of the moth-balled ships in the harbor, take the passenger-only ferry to Port Orchard. The **Naval Museum** is on the main street, just up the street from the ferry dock. Returning to Seattle, the ferry ride from Bremerton takes about an hour.

Information about the Olympic and Kitsap Peninsulas is available from the Seattle/King County Convention and Visitor Information Centers in the Seattle area. Also, there are local Chambers of Commerce and area information centers on the Olympic and Kitsap Peninsulas:

The Bainbridge Island Chamber of Commerce, 153 Madrone Lane, Winslow, 98110. Phone 1-842-3700.

The Bremerton/Kitsap County Visitor & Convention Bureau, 120 Washington Street, Bremerton, 98310. Phone 1-479-3588 or 1-479-3594.

The Port Angeles Visitor Center, 121 East Railroad, Port Angeles, 98362. Phone 1-452-2363.

Victoria

Victoria, the quaint town across the Canadian border, is famous for its gardens and English ambiance. It is full of pubs, shops, inns and tea houses in turn-of-the-century buildings.

For travellers going only to Victoria and not planning any further travel there is no need to take a car along. Victoria is a small village built around its U-shaped harbor and is easy to see by walking. Buses for sightseeing and the trip to Butchardt Gardens meet all arriving ships.

Getting to Victoria:

Going to Victoria is a case of "getting there is half the fun," but the trip does require some advance planning. Crossing the Canadian/American border is usually not difficult: Some proof of American citizenship, such as a driver's licence, voter's registration card, birth certificate, or passport, is required for adults and proof of identity may be required for children. For more detailed information, check with **Tourism British Columbia's** office in Seattle at 720 Olive Way, 9th floor; phone 623-5937. The office is closed, weekends, Canadian holidays and between 12-1pm daily.

Returning to the States, U.S. citizens are allowed $25 worth of articles per person for a stay of less than 48 hours and $400 if the stay has been 48 hours or longer. For more information, pick up a Customs booklet at the Visitors Information office or call 442-4676.

BC Stena Line

The *Princess Marguerite* and the *Vancouver Island Princess,* owned by the BC Stena Line, sail daily from Pier 48. The trip takes approximately four and a half hours. For walk-on passengers reservations are advised, but not required. The *Princess Marguerite* is passengers-only;

reservations are required for vehicles on the *Island Princess*. A Scandinavian buffet is available on each trip. There is also a snack shop, souvenir shop, video arcade and a lounge with entertainment and gambling.

Personal checks not accepted.

Cost:	Summer: Adult, $29 one-way, $39 round-trip; seniors, $25 one-way, $34 round-trip; children 5-15, $14 one-way, $19 round-trip. Auto & driver, $49 each way. Lower rates off-season.
Hours:	Departs Seattle: summer, 8am & 10am; winter, 10am.
Phone:	441-5560.

The Victoria Clipper

The catamaran *Victoria Clipper* departs from Pier 69 and takes 2 1/2 hours to go to Victoria. It is passengers-only, no cars; reservations are required. A "cold" buffet, available for breakfast or dinner, costs about $5.00.

Cost:	Adult, $42 one-way, $69 round-trip; seniors and children, $36 one-way, $59 round-trip.
Hours:	Departs Seattle: summer, 8:30am & 3:30pm; winter, 3pm.
Phone:	448-5000.

Driving/Ferry Combinations:

For a scenic, longer journey to Victoria, take one of the Washington State Ferries across Puget

Sound and sightsee en route to Port Angeles, where the **Black Ball Ferry** departs for Victoria. Allow about three hours travelling time from downtown Seattle to Port Angeles. Ferry schedules are available at many places, including the Visitor Information offices, hotels, and the Washington State Ferry terminal at Pier 52.

The **Seattle-Winslow ferry** leaves from Pier 52, takes 35 minutes, and has frequent departures. There's also the **Keystone-Port Townsend ferry.** The Port Angeles-Victoria ferry trip takes 1 hour and 35 minutes and makes four trips daily during the summer. Reservations are not accepted. If taking a car, arrive early to be sure of getting on. There's cafeteria service on all ferries. Also see Ferries, page 87.

Seattle-Winslow Ferry

Cost: Car & driver, $5.55 ($6.55 summers); passengers and walk-ons, $3.30 one-way OR round-trip; children & seniors, $1.65 one way.

The Black Ball Ferry

Hours: Summer: 4 round-trips daily; winter: 2 trips daily.

Cost: $22 ($U.S.) for car and driver; $5.50 for passengers or walk-ons, one way.

Phone: 622-2222.

There are two other water routes to Victoria, one from the U.S. and one from Canada. The scenery on both trips is spectacular.

Anacortes-Sidney Ferry

The Anacortes-Sidney Ferry departs from Anacortes and stops at the San Juan Islands along the way to Sidney, B.C.; the trip takes three hours. During the summer months reservations may be made for this ferry trip.

Driving to Anacortes from Seattle: Go north on I-5 to the Anacortes sign, exit #226 (Mt. Vernon), and head west to Anacortes, approximately 1 hour 45 minutes from Seattle to the ferry dock.

Cost:	$26.05 ($31.25 summer), car and driver, one way. Passengers: $6.05, adults; $3.05, children & seniors.
Phone:	464-6400.

BC Ferries

To the north, Canada's BC Ferries depart from Tsawwassen, southwest of Vancouver, and go through the Gulf Islands to Swartz Bay, just north of Sidney. The drive from Seattle to Tsawwassen takes approximately 2 3/4 hours with a normal border crossing. The ferry trip from Tsawwassen to Swartz Bay takes 1 hour 35 minutes, and the drive from Sidney south to Victoria takes approximately 45 minutes. Ferries leave hourly during the summer, less frequently other times; no reservations. Food and cafeteria service available on all ferries.

Cost:	$21 Canadian (about $18.80 U.S), car and driver; $4.50 Canadian (about $3.60 U.S), passenger, one-way. Both U.S. and Canadian money is accepted.
Phone:	441-6865 or (604) 656-0757.

Seaplane:

The fastest way to get to Victoria from downtown Seattle is by a seaplane from Lake Union. The planes land right in Victoria's inner harbor. Flight time is approximately 45 minutes.

Lake Union Air Service

Lake Union Air Service has six regularly scheduled flights daily in the summer. Reservations required.

Cost: $99 round-trip, $54 one-way.

Phone: 284-0300.

Kenmore Air

Kenmore Air has charter plane service; reservations required.

Cost: $225 for one to three people, one-way.

Phone: 364-1257.

Airplane:

Three airlines have service from Sea-Tac Airport to Victoria with a variety of schedules and prices: **Air BC**, phone 1-800-663-0522; **San Juan Airlines**, phone 1-800-241-6522; and **Canadian Air,** phone 1-800-426-7000.

Bus:

Bus transportation between Seattle and Anacortes is available. **Evergreen Trails/Gray Line** buses go from Sea-Tac Airport and downtown Seattle to the Anacortes ferry dock early every morning.

Phone: 626-6090 or 1-800-528-0447.

Whidbey Island

Whidbey Island's quiet charm makes it an ideal getaway spot for a short visit or a long vacation. The drive along its rolling hills offers views of the countryside, historic sites and the water on both sides of the island. The southern part of Whidbey, the longest island in the contiguous United States, is rural and arty while the north end is more densely populated. A visit to one of the island's many bed and breakfast inns is a good way to soak up Whidbey's bucolic scenery.

The free public transit system runs the length of the island, from the Clinton ferry landing in the south to Oak Harbor at the north end, making stops at the towns and Keystone ferry dock in between. To ride, wait at a bus stop and flag the bus down as it approaches. Buses come every hour weekdays, on a limited schedule Saturdays, and do not run on Sundays and holidays. Call **Whidbey Island Transit,** 1-678-7771, for information.

The short ferry trip from Mukilteo disembarks at **Clinton** on the southeast end of Whidbey. The main road, Hwy 525, heads north from the ferry landing. A helpful, detailed map of the island is available at the Visitors' Information office in the shopping complex on the right a couple of miles from the ferry dock. Note: Highway signs are rare; check your maps before starting out and look for regular street signs to your destination.

The picturesque town of **Langley** is about 20 minutes' drive northeast of Clinton on Langley Road. Besides its views and waterfront park, Langley has attractive shops with merchandise reflecting the artistic talents of the area's residents.

To continue north, return to Hwy 525 by way of **Bayview**, pausing at **Freeland** for a stop at the bakery on the main street. In addition to baked goods, the bakery sells picnic lunches perfect for eating later at one of the many scenic spots on the island.

Approaching **Greenbank**, on the right just south of the Greenbank Store on Resort Road is a sign for the **Meerkert Rhododendron Gardens.** They are open year-round Wednesday-Sunday, 9am-4pm, and are especially beautiful in the spring when the rhododendrons are in bloom. The island's narrowest spot is Greenbank, known for its legendary loganberries. Whidbey's Greenbank Farm produces its liqueur from these berries, reputed to be the best, not only on the island but in the world. The farm, owned by the same company that owns Ste. Michelle Winery, is open for self-guided tours and wine, but not liqueur, tastings. It also has a gift shop and restrooms. The building and grounds are meticulously clean.

The Mukilteo lighthouse

Whidbey's Greenbank Farm

Hours: 10am-4:30pm, daily.

Cost: Free.

A few miles north of Greenbank the well-marked road to the **Keystone Ferry** landing and **Fort Casey State Park** branches off to the west. To go to the park, continue past the underwater preserve and around Crockett Lake to the park's entrance. Fort Casey's gun emplacements and **Admiralty Head lighthouse** recall Whidbey Island's past at the turn of the century when it was part of the defense triangle on Puget Sound. Fort Casey has picnic and camping areas, as well as public restrooms.

Fort Casey Tours

Hours: 2pm, Sat. and Sun. only.

Cost: Free.

Coupeville's historic Victorian homes, wharf and museum reflect the town's importance in the 19th century. The National Park Service exhibit at the foot of the wharf and the **Island County Historical Society Museum** (call for hours, 1-678-6854), just off Front Street, have information about the area's history. **Captain Whidbey's Inn**, one of the island's landmarks, is about three miles west of Coupeville, along Madrona Way.

Oak Harbor's proximity to the U.S. Navy Air Station has made it the island's largest city. A large Dutch windmill sits on the public beach in the heart of town.

North of Oak Harbor, the road climbs into the woods and in a few minutes there are turn-offs for the parks, trails and campgrounds around **Deception Pass.** Pedestrians may cross the bridge to see spectacular views of the tidal currents below.

For **Visitor Information** contact the Whidbey Island Visitors Council, P.O. Box 809, Coupe-

ville, WA 98239. Phone: 1-678-5305. Also,
visitor information in the towns is available
through the local Chambers of Commerce or
privately operated concerns.

La Conner

La Conner, a small picturesque waterfront
town with 19th-century ambiance, is a few miles'
detour on the way from Deception Pass heading
east to I-5. Country shops and restaurants from
casual to the more elegant **Black Swan** line the
Swinomish Slough. For a look at the area's history, visit the restored Victorian **Gaches Mansion**
on Second Street, open Fridays-Sundays and the
Historical Museum on Fourth Street open Wed-
nesdays-Sundays. Visitor information is available
at the Chamber of Commerce office on First
Street in the Lime Dock building; phone
1-466-4778.

The San Juan Islands

The San Juan Islands, known for their un-
spoiled beauty, are one of Washington's most
popular areas to visit in the summer. Many people
explore the islands by boat, which enables them to
search out secluded harbors and beaches. Others
take a Washington State Ferry from Anacortes
that stops at Lopez, Shaw, Orcas, and San Juan (at
Friday Harbor) islands. The ferry trip is full of
beautiful views of the smaller islands and sea life;
whales may be seen swimming nearby.

During the summer, visitors overwhelm the
ferry system and long waits are the norm, especially for passengers travelling with cars. Riders are
advised to arrive at least an hour before the ferry's
departure time, and even earlier on weekends.
Driving time from Seattle to the Anacortes ferry
dock is approximately 1 3/4 hours. Only the international ferry from Anacortes to Sydney, B.C. ac-
cepts reservations, but only in the summer; phone
1-800-542-7052 from Washington or 206-464-
6400 from out of state. See the section on Ferries,
page 97, for more ferry information.

The first stop on most trips is **Lopez Island**, a
favorite with bicyclists because of its gentle terrain. In between the few shops near the ferry landing and the historic Richardson General Store at
the opposite end of the island, there are some bed
and breakfast inns and the beautiful rural land-
scape to enjoy.

Shaw Island, the quietest of the San Juan
islands with ferry service, has few public
facilities. There is a store by the ferry dock—the
dock is operated by nuns—and a public beach at
Shaw Island County Park.

In contrast, public parks and tourist facilities
abound on horseshoe-shaped **Orcas Island**. The
road from the ferry landing goes in a half-circle to
Eastsound in the middle and down the other side
to **Olga**. Orcas has arts and crafts of all types in

galleries and shops. The Artworks, in Olga, is a former strawberry processing plant turned into a cooperative of local artists.

The road goes through **Moran State Park**, named after the industrialist who donated the land for the park and built what is now the Rosario resort. Inside the park, the road branches to the left and goes six miles up **Mt. Constitution**, at 2,409 feet the highest spot in the islands—a wonderful spot for views. The twisty road makes for a scenic drive or a grueling bicycle ride.

Friday Harbor, the islands' largest town, is nestled around the San Juan Island ferry landing, making it easy to visit without a car. There are many shops, restaurants and galleries on the main street just beyond the dock and the **Whale Museum** is on First Street, within walking distance of the ferry dock.

Whale Museum

Hours:	11am-4pm daily; 10am-5pm, summer.
Cost:	Adults, $2.50; teens & seniors, $2; under 12, $1; under 5, free.
Phone:	1-378-4710.

The public **Whale Watching Park** is on the west side of the island, a 20-minute drive from Friday Harbor, and several whale watching cruises are available.

Picturesque **Roche Harbor**, also on San Juan Island, with its historic **Hotel de Haro** and gardens is on the northwest coast approximately a half-hour drive from Friday Harbor. Nearby **English Camp**, a tranquil cove named for the troops quartered there in the mid-nineteenth century, is now a national park, as is its counterpart at the south end of the island, **American Camp**, where the opposing American troops were

bivouacked. The troops faced off once in a skir-
mish referred to as the "**Pig War**," in honor of its
only casualty, as the countries debated the islands'
ownership. In 1872 the lower islands became the
American San Juans and the northern islands,
Canada's Gulf Islands. The National Park Service
presents programs at both English Camp and
American Camp during the summer.

A word of warning: The San Juans' rural at-
mosphere belies their popularity. Plan ahead and
make reservations if you plan to stay overnight on
the islands.

Water Tour

Grayline's narrated **San Juan Island Cruise**
departs from the Semiahmoo Resort north of
Bellingham and tours around the islands.

Cost:	Adults, $32; children 5-12, $16.
Phone:	441-1887.

Getting to the San Juan Islands

In addition to the Washington State Ferries,
two private ferry companies have service to the
San Juans during the summer. The **Redhead,**
phone 1-385-5288, makes daily trips between the
Point Hudson Marina in Port Townsend and the
Friday Harbor ferry dock. The **San Juan Ferry,**
operated by **A.I.T. Waterways**, phone 1-733-
9440, sails daily from Bellingham, stopping first
on Orcas Island at Leiberhaven near Obstruction
Pass and then at Friday Harbor on San Juan
Island. Both are passenger-only. See the Ferry
section, page 89, for more information.

Plane service to the islands is available:
San Juan Airlines, phone 1-800-241-6522,
has scheduled flights to the islands. **Lake Union
Air**, in downtown Seattle, provides regular seaplane service to the islands; call 284-0300. **Ken-**

more Air, phone 364-1257, and **Chartair**, phone 1-378-3133, provide charter service to the islands.

Information about the San Juan Islands is available from Visitor Information Offices on Lopez Island, 1-468-3800; Orcas Island, 1-376-2273; San Juan Island, 1-378-5240; and the San Juan Islands Tourism Cooperative, phone 1-468-3663.

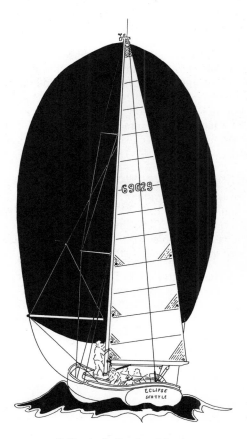

Sailing in the San Juan Islands

Leavenworth

Leavenworth turned itself into a Bavarian Village in the '60s when it decided to capitalize on its gorgeous physical setting. The Bavarian theme is pervasive, from the "Wilkommen zu Leavenworth" sign on the road, to the Bavarian style architecture, the oom-pah music in the streets, and merchandise for sale, making it a festive place to visit. In addition, there are several theme festivals during the year, such as the **Autumn Leaf Festival**, the **Christmas Lighting Festival** and the **MaiFest.**

With its outstanding location, the Leavenworth area is the center for many outdoor activities, such as river rafting, fishing, rock climbing and cross-country skiing.

For more information, contact the Leavenworth Chamber of Commerce, P.O. Box 327, 703 Highway 2, Leavenworth, WA 98826. Phone: 509-548-5807.

Getting to Leavenworth:

From Seattle, head north on I-5 and take the Bothell/Lake City Exit, #171. That becomes Hwy 522; continue on 522 following the signs to Stevens Pass. Leavenworth is 115 miles northeast of Seattle, approximately three hours' driving time.

PART II

And More

The first chapters of **The Pocket Guide** covered Seattle by areas (one reader described it as "expanding concentric circles"), since people often think in terms of a time frame, distance, or area when they sightsee.

Another approach is to think in terms of categories, such as visiting museums, wineries or beaches. This last section takes that approach with Seattle's attractions. It also includes many special needs, such as interpreters, medical care and currency exchange. As in the earlier sections, boldface names are listed in the index.

Airport Transportation

Regular service is available from Seattle's Sea-Tac International Airport to surrounding areas on Metro and several shuttle services. All, unless noted, leave from Sea-Tac's lower level and stop first at the side parking lot at the north end of the airport beyond United's baggage carousel #16 and make a second stop five minutes later outside of baggage carousel #1. Reservations are recommended. For ground transportation information, call Sea-Tac's **Skyline** 431-4444 or toll-free: 1-800-544-1965. Phone the carriers for specific schedule and fare information.

SEATTLE AND NORTH:

Metro

Metro buses #174 & 194 go between Sea-Tac Airport and downtown Seattle. They depart from in front of the parking lot at the south end of the airport. Passengers with bulky baggage may be refused.

Cost: $.85 non-peak hours;
                $1.25 peak hours (6am-
                9am & 3pm-6pm).

Phone: 447-4800.

Seattle Gray Line Airporter

The bus goes between Sea-Tac Airport and the major downtown hotels. Departs approximately every 15 minutes from 5am to midnight from the Gray Line booths on the road in front of the airport on the baggage level at baggage carousel #16 at the north end and #3 at the south end.

Cost: $5.50 one-way.

Phone: 626-6088.

The Shuttle Express

The van goes between Sea-Tac Airport and anywhere within 30 miles of the airport. Passengers must call for service with pick-up and drop-off information.

Cost: $9 and up, one-way,
                depending on distance.

Phone: 1-800-942-1711, or
                286-4800.

Greyhound

Goes between Sea-Tac Airport and the downtown Seattle Greyhound depot at 9th Avenue and Stewart. Buses leave from the south end of the airport, on the sidewalk in front of baggage carousel #1.

Cost: $2.50 one-way.

Phone: 624-3456.

The Everett Airporter (EASE)

Goes between Sea-Tac Airport and Everett with stops in the University District, Northgate, Lynnwood, and South Everett.

Cost: $7-$11 one-way, depend-
                         ing on distance.

Phone: 743-3344.

The Bellingham Airporter

Goes between Sea-Tac Airport and Bellingham with stops in Marysville, Stanwood, Mt. Vernon and Semiahmoo.

Cost: $12-$25 one-way, depend-
                         ing on distance.

Phone: 1-800-BELLAIR.

BELLEVUE AND THE EAST SIDE:

Metro

Bus #340 goes between Sea-Tac Airport and Bellevue. It departs from in front of the parking lot at the south end of the airport, beyond baggage carousel #1. Passengers with bulky baggage may be refused.

Cost: $.85 non-peak hours;
                         $1.25 peak hours (6am-
                         9am & 3pm-6pm).

Phone: 447-4800.

The Suburban Airporter

Goes between Sea-Tac Airport and Redmond, making stops at Bellevue, Kirkland, and Totem Lake, with other stops arranged.

Cost: $7.50-$12 one-way, depending on distance.

Phone: 455-2353.

Anacortes Sea-Tac Airporter

Goes between Sea-Tac Airport and the Anacortes ferry dock with stops in the town of Anacortes. Reservations required.

Cost: $20 one-way.

Phone: 293-8443.

VANCOUVER, B.C.:

The Quick As Air (Maverick)

Goes between Sea-Tac Airport and Vancouver, B.C., in 3 1/2 hours and makes four stops in Vancouver. First stop at Sea-Tac is by the Gray Line booth in front of the airport.

Cost: $26 one-way.

Phone: (604) 255-1171.

Greyhound

Goes between Sea-Tac Airport and the Vancouver Greyhound depot, 150 Dunsmuire Street, with stops in Seattle and other cities depending upon the bus.

Cost: $19.95 one-way.

Phone: 624-3456.

BREMERTON-KITSAP PENINSULA:

The Bremerton-Kitsap Airporter

Goes between Sea-Tac Airport and northwest Tacoma by way of Poulsbo, Bangor, Silverdale, Bremerton, Port Orchard, Purdy and Gig Harbor.

Cost: $10-$20 one-way, depending on distance.

Phone: 876-1737.

TACOMA AND OLYMPIA:

Capital Airporter

Goes between Sea-Tac Airport and Olympia with stops in Centralia, Chehalis and Shelton.

Cost: $17-$23 one-way, depending on distance.

Phone: 1-572-9544.

Travelines/Tacoma Airport Shuttle

Goes between Sea-Tac Airport and downtown Tacoma with stops in Fife, and at the Doric and Sheraton (Tacoma) Hotels.

Cost: $8-$10 one-way, depending on distance.

Phone: 1-839-2886 or 841-8196.

Ft. Lewis-McChord Airporter

Goes between Sea-Tac Airport and Ft. Lewis with stops at Madigan Hospital and McChord A.F.B.

Cost: $7-$8, one-way, depending on distance.

Phone: 876-1737.

Amusement Parks

Seattle Center's **Fun Forest** is the only permanent amusement park in Seattle. The rides and booths open at noon and operate until midnight daily during the summer; they are open weekends during the spring and fall, depending upon the weather. The prices vary, depending upon the ride or game; entrance is free.

Hours: Noon-midnight (summer).

Phone: 684-7200.

Enchanted Village, approximately a half hour south of Seattle on I-5, charges an entry fee into the park that includes the rides. It is possible to buy a combination ticket for Enchanted Village and **Wild Waves Water Park**, which is adjacent. Both are open only in the summer from 10am-7pm; later on weekends.

Hours: 10am-7pm (summer).

Phone: 838-1700.

Currency Exchange

The main branches of downtown banks will exchange U.S. money for foreign currencies or vice versa; most banks are able to exchange Canadian-U.S. dollars.

Deak International, phone 623-6203, with locations in downtown Seattle and Bellevue, can exchange several currencies. The downtown office is open weekdays only and the Bellevue office is also open on Saturdays.

The **Mutual of Omaha booth at Sea-Tac Airport,** phone 243-1231, located behind the American Airlines ticket counter, acts as a foreign exchange service and is open daily from 6am-9pm.

Some hotels will exchange currency depending upon their supply.

Ferries

The Washington State Ferry system is the largest in the nation, which is not surprising with all the water on the western side of the state. While riding a ferry is part of the daily commute for many Washingtonians, it is also an excellent way for visitors to get out on the water and see some of Washington's beautiful scenery.

To ride a ferry as a walk-on passenger, be at the ferry terminal 10-15 minutes before departure, buy a ticket and walk on when the ferry is ready. Passengers pay only on the Seattle side.

To go with a vehicle, allow more time, especially on weekends and during commuter hours. Vehicles are loaded in order of arrival; once your car is in line you can go explore the waterfront. There are no reservations on Washington State Ferries except on the Anacortes-Sydney ferry during the summer (see the Victoria section, page 71). Some of the private ferries accept reservations.

Two ferries leave from **Pier 52** on the Seattle waterfront. The trip to **Winslow** is aboard one of the jumbo ferries, the newest and largest in the fleet. Ferries between Seattle and Winslow leave approximately every hour. The crossing takes 35 minutes, a round-trip takes about 1 1/2 hours. Ferries between Seattle and **Bremerton** are slightly less frequent; the crossing takes one hour, a round-trip takes about 2 1/2 hours. The ferries are large and comfortable and offer cafeteria service.

The terminal has a small restaurant, bar, T-shirt shop, and very small restrooms; a McDonald's is below on the street level. The beautiful old clock from the original Colman dock is on display; plans are to install it in the new ferry terminal when it is built. The **information desk** in the terminal is open from 7:30am to 6:30pm. Ferry schedules are available at the terminal and Visitor Information Centers throughout the Seattle area.

CROSS SOUND FERRIES:

Cost: Passengers, one way OR round trip, $3.30; children 5-11 and seniors, $1.65. Auto & driver, $6.65 EACH way. Fares are higher in the summer.

Phone: 464-6400 or 1-800-542-7052. For recorded schedule information call 624-4500, then 2840 from a touchtone phone.

Washington State Ferry routes for other ferries are shown on most Washington State maps. All the ferry trips are scenic with views of Puget

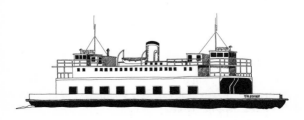

The Washington State Ferry Vashon

Sound and its islands, but the most popular is the trip through the **San Juan Islands**. Ferries depart from **Anacortes,** approximately 1 3/4 hours' drive north and west of Seattle, and sail to four of the islands. Extra sailings are added for the peak season. Allow plenty of time; the ferries are jammed in the summer, especially on weekends.

Prices:	Vary depending upon destination.
Phone:	464-6400 or 1-800-542-7052. For recorded schedule phone information call 624-4500, then 2840 from a touchtone phone.

PRIVATE FERRY LINES:

In addition to the state ferry system several private lines serve other communities.

Port Townsend - Friday Harbor

The **Redhead,** a small, passenger-only ferry, docks on the north side of Port Townsend's Point Hudson Marina. It departs in the mornings for the ferry dock on Friday Harbor on San Juan Island, returning to Port Townsend in the afternoon. Sailings are daily during the summer, May through September. Reservations are accepted and recommended. A box lunch may be ordered at the same time. Coffee and rolls available on the morning sailing.

Cost:	$25.50 round-trip; $18 one way.
Phone:	1-385-5288.

Bellingham - San Juan Islands

The **San Juan Ferry**, operated by **A.I.T. Waterways**, sails daily during the summer from

Bellingham to Leiberhaven near Obstruction Pass
on Orcas Island and Friday Harbor. Departure
hours vary; call for schedule and/or to make reservations. Passengers and limited freight only.

Cost: $20 round-trip; $14 one
                      way.

Phone: 733-9440.

Bremerton - Port Orchard

Washington's shortest ferry trip is the ten-
minute journey between Bremerton and Port Orchard. The boat departs at quarter to and quarter
past the hour from its dock just across the parking
lot from the Seattle-Bremerton ferry dock. Passengers and bicycles only.

Cost: $.60 each way.

Seattle - Victoria

For information on ferry service to **Victoria,
B.C.**–the *Victoria Clipper*, **BC Stena Line's** *Princess Marguerite* and *Vancouver Island Princess*,
from Seattle, and **Black Ball's** ferry from Port Angeles–see the section on Victoria, pages 65-68.

Seattle - Alaska

The ferry sails from Seattle to Alaska on
Fridays departing from the **Alaska Marine Highway terminal, Pier 48,** on Alaskan Way. Starting
1990 Alaskan ferries will move to Bellingham.
Reservations required; call 623-1149 or 1-800-
642-0066.

Contact a travel agent for information on cruise
ships going to Alaska.

Fish

For those who want to buy some of Washington's
celebrated seafood, there are several fisharkets in the

Pike Place Market and also many throughout the greater Seattle area listed in the Yellow Pages under "Fish." Most will pack fresh seafood to travel. Note: It's a good idea to carry perishable items with you on planes rather than checking them with the luggage.

Fishing

A **license** is required for persons 16-69 to fish for most species in Washington. The Department of Wildlife issues licenses for inland waters and the Department of Fisheries issues licenses for saltwater species. Both licenses may be purchased at many drug, hardware, and sporting goods stores. Prices vary depending on residency, time period, and species.

For information call the Washington State Department of Fisheries: 1-586-1425, or the Washington Department of Wildlife: 1-753-5700.

Gardens

With Seattle's mild, moist climate, plants and flowers flourish. Below is a list of some favorite public gardens.

Woodland Park Rose Garden adjacent to the Woodland Park Zoo, page 43.

The **University of Washington** campus; the roses by the **Drumheller fountain,** page 44.

Carl S. English, Jr. Gardens at the Locks, page 37.

The **Washington Park Arboretum,** page 46.

The **Japanese Garden** in the Arboretum, page 47.

The grounds of **Seattle Center,** pages 28-33.

Volunteer Park;

the **Conservatory**;
the **dahlia** (Seattle's official flower) display
southeast of the Conservatory.

The **Herbfarm** in Fall City.

The **Bloedel Reserve** on Bainbridge Island.
Open Wednesday through Sunday. Phone
1-842-7631 for reservations and directions.

Interpreters/ Language Bank

The American Red Cross provides volunteer
interpreters who are able to translate 70 languages
and dialects for people needing assistance. Volunteers are available 24 hours a day through the Red
Cross Language Bank.

Phone: 323-2345.

Medical Care

For emergencies, call 911.

Medical care is available through area hospitals and organizations.

Hospital emergency rooms throughout the
greater Seattle area are open 24 hours a day for
emergencies. Several hospitals are located just outside the downtown area; check the Yellow Pages
listings under "Hospitals."

For less traumatic illnesses, there are clinics
and medical centers. Hours and prices vary; it's a
good idea to call beforehand to be sure they can
meet your needs.

The **Downtown Clinic**, Medical Dental Building
at 5th and Olive, Suite 1664, in downtown Seattle.

Hours: Monday-Friday, 8am-5pm; Saturday, 9am-1pm. Phone 682-3808.

CarePlus Medical Centers have several locations. The two nearest to downtown Seattle are in West Seattle, phone 932- 4321, and 147th and Aurora Avenue, phone 365-0220.

CHEC Medical Centers have several locations throughout the greater Seattle area. In downtown Seattle there is a clinic at Denny and Fairview Avenue. Phone 682-7418.

Museums

There are many museums in the greater Seattle area, each specializing in some aspect of art, science or history. Most are closed one day a week (Monday usually) and most offer one day a week when admission is free. Many are tricky to find. Call to check on directions, hours, prices and exhibits. Unless noted, the museums are in Seattle.

In addition to the museums listed below, there are many galleries featuring works of art in all media. Pioneer Square has galleries tucked in its attractive older buildings. Check the Yellow Pages for listings and addresses.

Bellevue Art Museum
Third Floor, Bellevue Square, Bellevue

Permanent exhibit, plus changing shows. Gift shop.

Phone: 454-6021.

Bremerton Naval Museum
130 Washington Street, Bremerton

Ship models, naval weapons and artifacts.

Phone: 1-479-SHIP.

Burke Museum
Northwest corner, University of Washington

Northwest Native American and natural history exhibits. Gift store and coffee shop. See page 44.

Phone: 543-5590.

Coast Guard Museum
Pier 36, 1519 Alaskan Way South

History of Coast Guard in the Pacific Northwest. Free.

Phone: 286-9608.

Frye Art Museum
707 Terry Avenue

Permanent and changing exhibits.

Phone: 622-9250.

Henry Art Gallery
15th Avenue, University of Washington

Permanent and changing exhibits. Gift shop. See page 44.

Phone: 543-2280.

Klondike Museum
117 South Main Street, Pioneer Square

Exhibits and movies of Seattle's role in the Alaska Gold Rush. See page 22.

Phone: 442-7220.

Marymoor Museum
Marymoor Park, Redmond

History and crafts of the communities on the east side of Lake Washington.

Phone: 885-3684.

Museum of Flight
9404 East Marginal Way South

History and exhibits of flight. Gift shop. See page 49.

Phone: 764-5720.

Museum of History and Industry
2700 24th Avenue East (entrance is on the west side of Hwy 520)

Puget Sound history. Gift shop.

Phone: 324-1125.

Nordic Heritage Museum
3014 NW 67th Street

Exhibits depicting the Scandanavian heritage in Puget Sound. Gift shop.

Phone: 789-5707.

Pacific Science Center
200 2nd Avenue, Seattle Center

Hands-on exhibits, displays, movies and changing shows. Restaurant and gift shop. See page 31.

Phone: 443-2001.

Puget Sound Railway Historical Association
The Snoqualmie Railroad depot, Snoqualmie

Exhibit of railroad-related items. Phone for days/hours. See page 55.

Phone: 746-4025.

Seattle Art Museum
Volunteer Park, 14th East & East Prospect

Permanent exhibits, including jade, and changing shows. Gift shop. The SAM Modern Art Gallery at Seattle Center is closed.

Phone: 625-8900.

Seattle Children's Museum
Lower floor, Center House, Seattle Center

A hands-on neighborhood, plus changing shows. See page 30.

Phone: 441-1767.

Shoreline Historical Museum
175th Street & Linden Avenue North

Exhibits from the turn-of-the-century Shoreline area.

Phone: 542-7111.

Snoqualmie Valley Historical Museum
320 So. North Bend Boulevard, North Bend

Displays of Snoqualmie Valley and Snoqualmie Pass history and development. See page 55.

Phone: 1-888-3200.

Suquamish Museum
Highway 305 on the Olympic Peninsula, just west of the Agate Pass Bridge

Historical exhibits of Indians of Puget Sound. Gift shop. See page 61.

Phone: 1-598-3311.

Water Link
Pier 57, about halfway out

Exhibits about Puget Sound's maritime heritage.
See page 18.

Phone: 624-4975.

Wing Luke Asian Museum
407 7th Avenue South

Exhibits of Seattle's Asian heritage. Gift shop.
See page 26.

Phone: 623-5124.

Nightlife

Seattle has a lively performing arts scene, with
resident symphony, ballet, and opera companies,
as well as many theaters. For current information,
check the sources listed on pages 118-121 in
Other Sources. **Ticketmaster** sells tickets to area
concerts and events, phone 628-0888. Or, try getting half-price day-of-show theater tickets through
TicketTicket, 324-2744.

The **Seattle Arts Hotline**, phone 447-ARTS,
has recorded information about non-profit arts
organizations such as symphony orchestras,
theaters, and touring events.

For those looking for more casual entertainment, many places around Pioneer Square have
bands or performers. Other areas to try are the restaurants around the south end of Lake Union and
out by Shilshole. Also, most of the major hotels
have lounges with music or dancing.

Parks

Seattle's extensive park system includes parks
of all varieties: There are large city parks, such as
Seattle Center, Volunteer Park and the **Arboretum**; view parks along the waterfronts and on hill-
sides; **Gasworks**, a unique park created from an
industrial eyesore; and **Discovery Park**, a wilderness park, to name a few; and many small "pocket" parks.

The Park Department supports a broad range of
activities at various parks—everything from
pleasant walks and views to playing golf, renting
boats and classes.

For information, call the **Seattle Parks and
Recreation Department.**

Phone: 684-4075.

Shopping

Stores and boutiques abound in downtown
Seattle with everything from designer stores to
surplus materials. The three major department
stores, **Frederick and Nelson, Nordstrom** and
The Bon Marche, surround the southern Monorail terminal at **Westlake Mall**. Smaller specialty
shops line Fifth Avenue and the side streets south
to **Rainier Square** at University Street. (Note:
The walls of the Underground Concourse from
One Union Square to Rainier Square are covered
with historical photographs of Seattle.) There are
many boutique-type shops in **Pioneer Square** and
near the **Pike Place Market** on First Avenue. The
piers on the waterfront are chockablock with
souvenir shops. In addition, there are many shops
in the major office buildings and tucked in
amongst the buildings.

For shopping beyond downtown, in the **University of Washington area** there are shops and res-

taurants catering to the student population all along University Avenue, known locally as "**The Ave.**" The **University Bookstore,** one of the country's largest, is located between 44th and 45th Streets on University Avenue. **University Village** is a shopping complex east of the university. On **Capitol Hill,** shops and restaurants line Broadway, and the **Fremont District** is known for its funky shops, restaurants and bars.

There are three major **shopping malls** each about a half hour's drive from downtown Seattle. Each of the malls has the major department stores, many smaller stores, and several restaurants.

Northgate

Northgate was one of the country's first shopping centers. Head north on I-5 to the Northgate Way exit at 103rd St., exit #173; the mall is straight ahead.

Southcenter

Southcenter is not far from Sea-Tac Airport. Head south on I-5 and exit at the Southcenter exit, #154. The shopping center is on the east side of the freeway.

Bellevue Square

Bellevue Square caters to the affluent Eastside. Drive east on either SR 520 or I-90 and get off at the Bellevue Way exit (on SR 520 the sign says only "Bellevue"); follow Bellevue Way to downtown Bellevue. Bellevue Square covers the blocks between Bellevue Way and 100th Avenue and Eighth and Fourth Streets.

Gilman Village

Gilman Village in Issaquah is an attractive shopping "village" in a cluster of turn-of-the-century buildings. The small shops feature hand-crafted items, antiques, and boutiques; the restaurants feature homemade breads and soups.

Take I-90 heading east to the Front Street exit, #17, in Issaquah; turn right at the next intersection onto Gilman Boulevard, and continue about 1/4 mile to Gilman Village on the left.

Skiing (Downhill)

Seattle's gentle rains and moderate temperatures turn into snow storms at the higher elevations of the nearby mountain passes. Skiers flock to the Cascades from Thanksgiving to mid-April for the excellent, accessible skiing.

There are four ski areas less than an hour's drive on I-90 from downtown Seattle; all have night skiing, equipment rentals, lodge and restaurant facilities, but few overnight accommodations. A little farther away, some of the areas offer accommodations, and the areas on the east side of the Cascades boast about their dry snow. In addition, there are several areas for cross-country skiing and some have facilities for downhill, cross-country and **snowboarding**. Equipment rentals and lessons are available at most areas; call for info. For general ski information, call the Washington State Department of Tourism: 1-586-2088 or the Seattle/King County Visitor Information: 447-4240.

It's a good idea to call to confirm hours of operation and conditions. The **Cascade Snowline** has recorded information for all the ski areas in the Cascades, phone 634-0200. For current **highway conditions** in the Cascades from November through March phone: 1-976-ROAD (calls cost $.30), or 455-7900. Note: Reports often state that approved traction devices are required; these include all-weather tires, snow tires and studded tires. Occasionally, chains are required.

Listed ticket prices are for adult all-day tickets only. All areas offer different tickets for half-days, nights, and children.

Snoqualmie Pass

The Snoqualmie Pass areas are the closest to Seattle, approximately a one-hour drive east on I-90 from downtown Seattle. Snoqualmie, Ski Acres and Alpental are owned by one parent company and one lift ticket is good at all three areas. Night skiing is available every night but not at all three areas. On weekends a free bus shuttles skiers from one area to another. Each area has its own restaurants, rental services, ski schools and other amenities.

Snoqualmie Summit has gentle terrain and caters to beginner skiers.

Ski Acres has 1,020 feet of vertical drop and has a broad range of skiing.

Alpental, with 2,200 feet of vertical drop, has long, steep runs.

Cost:	$19, weekends; $11, weekdays.
Phone:	232-8182; ski report, 236-1600.

Pac West

Pac West is an independent area a little farther to the east on Snoqualmie Pass with a vertical drop of 1,143 feet of mostly intermediate terrain, full facilities and snowmaking. Open for both day and night skiing, Friday-Sunday.

Cost:	$16.00.
Phone:	462-7669.

Getting to Snoqualmie Pass

Bus service from downtown Seattle and surrounding areas is available Wednesday through Sunday. Call for information, 232-8210.

Driving directions: Head east on I-90 to exit #52 (West Summit) for Alpental and Snoqualmie or exit #53 (East Summit) for Ski Acres and Pac West.

Stevens Pass

Stevens Pass, on the road to Leavenworth, has an 1,800 foot vertical drop, extensive terrain, night skiing and full facilities. Driving time from Seattle is approximately 1 3/4 hours.

Cost:	$22 weekends; $11, Wed.-Fri.; and $7, Mon. & Tues.
Phone:	1-973-2441; ski report, 634-1645.

Getting to Stevens Pass

From downtown Seattle, go across Lake Washington and head north on I-405 to the Monroe/Wenatchee exit, #23, and continue east on SR 2.

Crystal Mountain

Crystal Mountain Washington's largest ski area, has a 3,100 foot vertical drop, two new quad chairlifts, and extensive, varied terrain. On a clear day the view of Mt. Rainier is breathtaking. It has full facilities and some overnight accommodations. Limited night skiing.

Cost:	$24, Wed.-Sun.; $14, Mon. & Tues.
Phone:	663-2265; ski report, 634-3771.

Getting to Crystal Mountain

The drive from Seattle takes 1 3/4 hours. Bus transportation is available from outlying areas to Crystal; phone 455-5505.

Driving directions: head southeast to Enumclaw (there are several roads) and continue east on Rte 410.

For information about other ski areas in Washington, phone 1-586-2088.

Skiing (Cross-Country)

Several areas have facilities for cross-country skiing.

Ski Acres

Ski Acres' cross-country area includes a Cross-Country Center, two tracks with areas lighted for night skiing and full facilities.

Cost: $5; or $7.50 with 2 round-trip chairlift rides.

Phone: 232-8182.

Pac West

Pac West has groomed cross-country trails in addition to its downhill runs. Open Friday-Sunday.

Cost: $5.00.

Phone: 462-7669.

Mountainholm

Mountainholm, a little farther east on I-90, has full cross-country facilities. It is open weekends and holidays.

Cost: $5.00.

Phone: 1-509-656-2346.

Driving directions: Head east from Seattle on I-90 to exit #70 (Easton), approximately 1 1/2 hours from downtown Seattle.

Crystal Mountain

Crystal Mountain has some terrain suitable for cross-country skiing. A one-ride lift ticket is available.

Cost: $5.00.

Phone: 1-663-2265.

Mt. Rainier

There are three marked trails from Paradise, and the Ski Touring Center at Longmire offers rentals, lessons and advice for areas around Mt. Rainier.

Cost: $5.00 park entrance fee.

Phone: 1-569-2283.

Leavenworth

The Bavarian village of Leavenworth east of the Stevens Pass area has skiing trails around the village as well as a cross-country track.

Cost: $5.00

Phone: 1-509-548-5983.

Spectator Sports

Seattle has teams for all seasons. For ticket information and game schedules, call the numbers listed. Tickets for most events are also available through Ticketmaster, phone 628-0888. Metro schedules extra buses for some events; for information, call Metro, 447-4800.

Seahawks

The Seahawks, Seattle's popular NFL football team, fill the Kingdome for their home games from August to December.

Phone: 827-9777.

Supersonics

Home games of the Supersonics, Seattle's NBA basketball team, are played in the Coliseum at

Seattle Center. The regular season runs November through April.

Phone: 281-5850.

Mariners

The Mariners, the Northwest's American League baseball team, play their home games in the Kingdome from April to October.

Phone: 628-3555.

Thunderbirds

The Thunderbirds compete against other young teams in the Western Hockey League. Games are played in the Seattle Center Arena from October to March.

Phone: 728-9121.

Tacoma Stars

The MISL Tacoma Stars play indoor soccer at the Tacoma Dome from November to April.

Phone: 467-8551.

University of Washington

University of Washington teams are top contenders in their divisions and UW football games in Husky Stadium are usually soldout. More than 200,000 spectators flock to the Montlake Cut on the first Saturday in May to watch the annual "**Opening Day**" crew races that precede the **Opening Day Boat Parade**.

University of Washington sports information:

Phone: 543-2200.

Longacres

Thoroughbreds race Wednesdays through Sundays at the beautifully landscaped Longacres Race Course in Renton from April to early October.

Phone: 226-3131.

Tours are available Saturday mornings during the summer months. For tour information, phone 285-2295.

Getting to Longacres

Driving directions: From Seattle, take I-5 heading south to exit #156 (Tukwila-Interurban). Turn left onto Interurban Avenue and head south for approximately 2 miles to Longacres Avenue (158th St.) on the left, at the second stoplight after crossing under the freeway overpass. Exit 157 also leads to the track.

Seafair

Seattle's annual Seafair festival culminates in the **unlimited hydroplane races** the first Sunday in August every summer. The race course is on Lake Washington south of the Mercer Island Floating Bridge. Thousands of people watch from boats on the water but Seward Park at the south end of Lake Washington is where the landlubbers go.

Cost: $10.00.

Phone: 623-7100.

Steam Trains

Railroads were critical to Seattle's development in the 19th century, providing a link for commerce between Seattle and the rest of the country. Several grand old trains from earlier days travel scenic routes during the summer months and on some holidays. Call for hours and prices.

The **Mt. Rainier Scenic Railroad** departs from the Elbe station east of Tacoma and Hwy 7 for a 1 1/2 hour trip accompanied by live music. Runs daily during the summer and on weekends in September. Phone 1-569-2588.

The **Snoqualmie Railroad**, operated by the **Puget Sound Railway Historical Association**, runs steam- and diesel-powered trains from the depots at North Bend's Railroad Park and the historical station in Snoqualmie. Round-trip takes approximately 1 1/4 hours. Weekends in the summer; Sunday only in April, May, September and October; plus Christmas trains. Phone: 1-888-3030 or 746-4025.

The **Lake Whatcom Railroad** train goes through forests and farmlands east of Sedro Woolley for a scenic 11-mile trip. Weekends in the summer plus Christmas trains. Phone: 1-595-2218.

For a short scenic trip (approximately 15 minutes) the **Pt. Defiance, Quinault & Klickitat RR** runs an authentic geared logging train through logging exhibits in **Pt. Defiance Park** outside of Tacoma. Weekends in the summer and has Christmas trains. Phone: 1-752-0047.

Totem Poles

Totem poles are part of the Northwest's Indian heritage. Here are some in and around Seattle:

Pioneer Square Park, the small triangular park at First Avenue and Yesler Street.

Occidental Park, on Occidental Avenue between Washington and Main Streets.

Alaska Square, the small park on the waterfront at the foot of Washington Street. See page 15.

The **Pacific Science Center**, at Seattle Center. See page 31.

Victor Steinbrueck Park, on the water side of the Pike Place Market overlooking Elliott Bay, at Virginia Street and Western Avenue.

The **Burke Museum**, 17th Avenue NE & NE 45th Street, on the University of Washington campus. See page 44.

At the east entrance of the **Montlake Cut** on the south bank; just north of the Museum of History and Industry's upper parking lot.

Daybreak Star Cultural Center in Discovery Park. See page 40.

The **Suquamish Roadside Park** on Rte 305 west of Winslow. See page 61.

Belvedere Viewpoint, Admiral Way at SW Olga Street in West Seattle.

Tillicum Village on Blake Island; see page 16.

Rte 202 in **Fall City**.

Tours

There are many tours to attractions and facilities. Some are free, while others have an admission charge. Availability may change, so call to verify before setting out.

Here's a list to get started:

The Arboretum
See page 46-47.

Boehm's Chocolates
Free tours during the summer months only. Call for information and reservations. 255 NE Gilman Boulevard, Issaquah, WA 98027.
Phone: 392-6652.

Boeing's Everett plant
See page 53.

Chateau Ste. Michelle Winery
See page 113.

Chinatown Tours
See page 27.

Chinatown Discovery Tours
See page 27.

Columbia Winery
See page 114.

Gray Line Tours
Tours to several areas. Call 626-5208.

The Herbfarm
See page 56.

The Kingdome
See page 25.

The Locks
See page 37-39.

Major Marine Tours
See page 16.

Pike Place Market
See page 11.

Rainier Brewery
See page 115.

Redhook Ale Brewery
See page 116.

Seattle Harbor Tours
See page 16.

Snoqualmie Winery
See page 115.

Tillicum Village Tours
See pages 16.

Underground Tours
See page 22.

University of Washington Campus
See page 44.

Views and Scenic Drives

Seattle is a city of views–of the mountains and the water, of sunrises and sunsets, on clear days and gray days–there are hundreds of spectacular views. But even on ordinary days, Seattle's natural beauty with its expansive vistas offers many splendid sights.

The following is a list of some good ideas, but everyone has favorites.

The top of the **Space Needle**. (See page 28.)

Columbia Center. It costs $3.75 for the highest, but quite limited, view in Seattle. Check in with the Security Desk at the 5th Avenue entrance. Phone: 386-5151.

The view from the back (water) side of **Pike Place Market**.

Victor Steinbrueck Park near the Market, overlooking Elliott Bay.

From on top of the new Mt. Baker tunnel at the west end of the I-90 floating bridge.

Kerry Park, the small park west of Queen Anne Avenue on Highland Drive; and a little farther west, **Betty Bowen Park** across from **Parsons Gardens.**

Many of streets on **Queen Anne,** especially **Olympic Way**.

Kobe Terrace, on Washington Street just west of the freeway in the International District.

The **University of Washington campus**; Rainier Vista from **Drumheller fountain.**

Drive along **Lake Washington Boulevard**–any of the parks along the way.

The two **Lake Washington floating bridges**.
(Avoid the commuter hours or you'll have a
longer view than you need.)

Volunteer Park. The view from the top of the
water tower in Volunteer Park is the most
panoramic in Seattle; open 7am-8:15pm.

Boren Park on 15th Avenue and Garfield Street,
northeast of Volunteer Park.

Roanoke Park at the intersection of Roanoke
Street and 10th Avenue overlooking Portage Bay.

Gasworks Park on Lake Union.

Ivar's Salmon House on Lake Union.

Magnolia Boulevard–views of Puget Sound and
the Olympic mountains.

Discovery Park from the paths and down by the
Daybreak Star Indian Cultural Center.

Shilshole Marina and **Golden Gardens Park**
north of the Locks.

There are several expansive views in **West Seattle** looking north to Seattle or west across Puget
Sound. The **Belvedere Viewpoint** on SW Admiral and SW Olga is on the main road into West
Seattle. On the north side, the **Hamilton Viewpoint** at California SW and SW Donald overlooks
Elliott Bay. **Alki Beach** runs along the entire
northwest side of West Seattle; a statue com-
memorating the founding of Seattle is on the
western end. The **Alki Point Lighthous**e sits on
the western tip and farther along Beach Drive is
Schmitz Viewpoint Park.

Water Activities

Water, water everywhere—and how to enjoy it. With all the rivers, sloughs, lakes and saltwater around Seattle, many activities revolve around the water. Here are some suggestions.

Beaches

Freshwater: Greenlake in Woodland Park; Seward Park, Madronna Park, and Madison Park on the west (Seattle) side of Lake Washington. Several parks along the Lake Washington waterfront in Kirkland and Bellevue on the east side of Lake Washington. Also Sammamish State Park on Lake Sammamish. Call the Bellevue Park Department, 462-6046, or the Kirkland Park Department, 828-1218, for information.

Saltwater: Alki Beach in West Seattle; Golden Gardens north of Shilshole Marina.

Also Saltwater State Park south of Des Moines. Call the Seattle Parks Department, phone 684-4075, for information.

Boats

Paddle a canoe to explore the area around the Arboretum and Foster Island. **Canoes** and **rowboats** are available from the University of Washington Water Activities Center near Husky Stadium on Lake Washington. Call 543-9433 for information.

The Outdoor Center on Lake Union rents **canoes** and **kayaks** and leads water tours of the lakes in the summer. Phone 281-9694. **Kayaks** are available from the Swallows' Nest near Gasworks Park on Lake Union. Phone 633-0408.

At Greenlake, there are **canoes, rowboats, paddleboats** and **sailboards** for rent. Phone 527-0171.

Windsurfing boards and lessons are available on Lake Union, at Greenlake, and in Kirkland. Check the Yellow Pages for listings.

Sailboats and **powerboats** are available from a

number of sources. Check ads in newspapers and
local boating papers available at nautical supply
shops; also ask yacht brokers on Lake Union and
at marinas. For boat charters at Whidbey Island or
in the San Juan Islands check with their Visitors
Information Centers.

Several operators have fishing boat charters
depending upon the season. Check with local
marinas, newspapers, the Yellow Pages, or sporting goods stores for information.

River rafting down rivers in wilderness areas
is an adventurous way to see some of Washington's most beautiful scenery and, possibly, bald
eagles. Several companies operate on both sides
of the Cascades; the Seattle and Eastside Yellow
Pages have listings under "Rafting."

Wineries and Breweries

Several Washington wineries and breweries are
located in or near Seattle and offer free tours
and/or tastings to the public.

WINERIES:

Chateau Ste. Michelle
One Stimson Lane, Woodinville, WA 98072

Chateau Ste. Michelle, the state's largest
winery, has a traditional-style winery chateau on
spacious grounds in Woodinville–a nice spot for a
picnic. The gift shop sells picnic provisions. It has
tours followed by tastings on a drop-in basis daily
from 10:30am-4:30pm.

Driving time from Seattle: approximately 45
minutes.

Phone: 488-1133.

Columbia Winery
14030 NE 145th Street, Woodinville, WA 98072

Columbia Winery is one of the state's oldest wineries. It recently moved to new quarters across the street from Chateau Ste. Michelle and is open daily from 10am-5pm for tours and tastings.

Driving time from Seattle: approximately 45 minutes.

Phone: 488-2776.

Covey Run
107 Central Way, Kirkland, WA 98033

Covey Run's tasting room in downtown Kirkland is open from noon-6pm weekdays, Fridays until 9pm.

Driving time from Seattle: approximately 30 minutes.

Phone: 828-3848.

French Creek Winery
177 132nd Avenue NE, Woodinville, WA 98072.

French Creek Winery, located a few miles north of Chateau Ste. Michelle in Woodinville, is open for tours and tastings daily from noon-5pm.

Driving time from Seattle, approximately 45 minutes.

Phone: 486-1900.

Paul Thomas Wines
1717 136th Place NE, Bellevue, WA 98005

Paul Thomas Wines originally made only fruit wines but has expanded into varietals. Open Friday and Saturday, noon-5pm for tastings and tours.

Driving time from Seattle, approximately 20 minutes.

Phone: 747-1008.

Snoqualmie Winery
1000 Winery Road, Snoqualmie, WA 98065

Snoqualmie Winery overlooks the Snoqualmie Valley and is a short drive from the Snoqualmie Falls exit on I-90. It is open for tours and tastings 10am-4:30pm daily.

Driving time from Seattle, apprx. 40 minutes.

Phone: 1-392-4000.

Staton Hills Winery
1910 Post Alley, Seattle, WA 98101

Staton Hills Winery's tasting room at the north end of the Pike Place Market is open Monday-Friday, noon-5pm; Saturday, 11am-6pm.

Phone: 443-8084.

BREWERIES:
Washington's biggest and best-known breweries, Rainier and Olympia, have been joined in recent years by several micro-breweries catering to local beer connoisseurs. Beers and ales are on tap at many taverns and restaurants and most breweries offer tours and tastings.

Rainier Brewing Company
3100 Airport Way South, Seattle, WA 98134

Rainier Brewery, alongside I-5 just south of downtown Seattle, is the big local brewery now owned by an Australian company. It is open for tours and tastings Monday-Friday, 1pm-6pm.

Phone: 622-2600.

Olympia Brewery
Tumwater, WA

The Pabst Brewing Company, which bought the local Olympia Brewery, produces several brands at its Tumwater brewery. Located just south of Olympia (take exit #103 from I-5), it has tours from 8am-4:30pm daily. Driving time from Seattle, approximately 1 1/2 hours.

Phone: 1-754-5212.

Redhook Ale Brewery
3400 Phinney Avenue N., Seattle, WA 98103

Redhook Ale, the largest of the micro-breweries, recently moved into new quarters in the Fremont district. It is open for tours and tastings of its ales on the half-hour; weekdays, 11am-5pm; weekends, 11am-4:30pm. The Trolleyman Pub next door is open later. Driving time from Seattle, approximately 15 minutes.

Phone: 548-8000.

Noggins
Third Floor, Westlake Mall, 4th Avenue & Pine

Noggins, an English-style brew-pub on the third floor of the new Westlake Center, makes its brews with imported English malts. Open 11am-11pm Monday-Saturday, and until 7pm Sundays. Noggins plans to open another brew-pub at 4142 Brooklyn Avenue in the University district in early spring 1989.

Phone: 682-BREW

Big Time Brewery & Alehouse
4133 University Way

Also in the University district is the Big Time Brewery & Alehouse. It serves three brews along with food. Open from 11:30am to 1:30am, Monday through Friday, and noon-1:30am on weekends.

Phone: 545-4509.

Hale's Ales, Ltd.
109 Central Way, Kirkland, WA 98033

Hale's Ales, Ltd. is next door to Covey Run in downtown Kirkland in the Kirkland Roaster and Alehouse complex. The small brewery is open for tours and tastings during working hours, weekdays, 8am-5pm. Driving time from Seattle, approximately 30 minutes.

Phone: 827-4359.

Liberty Malt
1432 Western Avenue

Liberty Malt, a brewing supplier, is scheduled to open a micro-brewery on its premises in the spring of 1989. It is located on the back side of the Market, just north of the Hillclimb.

Phone: 622-1880.

Other sources of information about Seattle

There is excellent information about Seattle available from many sources, including some that are supported by their membership or advertisers. The following list includes some resources.

The **Seattle/King County Convention and Visitors Bureau,** known as the SKCCVB or The Bureau:

The executive offices are at 1815 Seventh Avenue, Seattle, 98101, until the spring of 1989 when it plans to move to the 520 Pike Building, Suite 1300, Seattle, 98101.

Phone: 447-4200.

Its main Visitor Information office: corner Seventh Avenue and Stewart Street.

Phone: 447-4240

Information Booth at Sea-Tac Airport by baggage carousel #9.

Phone: 433-5218.

Information booth at Seattle Center across from the Monorail ramp, open summer only.

Phone: 447-4244.

The Bureau publishes several booklets: Its excellent *Events Calendar* lists Seattle's attractions in addition to events for the 4-6 months covered by the booklet; it also publishes a *Visitors Guide* and a *Lodging Guide*.

The Bureau will mail out requested information–it has an abundance of material about Seattle and Washington.

The **East King County Convention and Visitors Bureau**, located just off I-405's NE 4th Street exit at 515 116th Avenue NE, Bellevue,

WA, 98004, has staff to answer inquiries. It publishes the *East King County Visitors Guide,* a quarterly booklet about Eastside attractions.

Phone: 455-1926.

The **South King County Convention and Visitors Bureau** serves the area south of Seattle from two locations: 15030 8th Avenue SW and 225 Tukwila Parkway.

Phone: 244-3160.

The Washington State Department of Tourism publishes *Destination Washington* which has visitor information for the entire state with the locations and phone numbers of the various visitor information centers.

Phone: 1-800-544-1800 for a free
                       copy; allow 3-4 weeks for
                       delivery.

The *Seattle Guide,* available in many hotel rooms and Visitor Information Centers, has current events, a list of restaurants, and general info.

The *Guest Informant,* available in many hotel rooms, emphasizes shopping opportunities in and around Seattle.

The Seattle Arts Commission booklet, *Seattle's Public Art,* is a guide to the many public works of art in and around Seattle. The illustrated booklet is available by mail or in person from their office in Center House, Seattle Center, 305 Harrison Street, Seattle, 98109. Phone: 684-7171.

Foreign Language Information

Some foreign language brochures and guide books, such as the *Pacific Companion* (Japanese) are available at SKCCVB Information Centers. The Visitor Information Booth by baggage carousel #1 at Sea-Tac Airport is staffed by Japanese-

speaking personnel; open 9:30am-1:30pm daily;
phone 433-4679. For more information, call the
Consulates.

British Columbia and Canada Information

The **Tourism British Columbia** office has information about British Columbia and Canada. Offices are on the 9th floor of the Marsh & McClel-
lan building at 720 Olive Way, Seattle. Phone
623-5937. Note: Office is closed from 1-2pm and
on weekends and Canadian holidays.

Newspapers

The Friday and Saturday editions of the Seattle *Time*s and the *Post-Intelligencer* and the sub-
urban papers have the most accurate and extensive information about current happenings as well
as restaurant reviews.

The Weekly has excellent current events information.

Magazines

Pacific Northwest lists many interesting restaurants in the Pacific Northwest area.

Washington, with its beautiful photographs,
has historical and travel pieces about the state.

Books

Seattle Best Places, by David Brewster, is the
classic. It rates restaurants and hotels and has extensive information about Seattle. Published every
two years.

Also Brewster's *Northwest Best Places* in the
same format.

The Seattle GuideBook by Archie Satterfield
is another comprehensive book with in-depth information about Seattle.

Discover Seattle with Kids by Rosanne Cohn
has ideas for children's activities.

The *Seattle Rainy Day Guide* by Clifford

Burke has suggestions for what to do on typical Seattle days.

Barry and Hilda Anderson's ***Pacific Northwest***, one of the World of Travel Publications books, has information about sights and trips in the Northwest, including British Columbia and southeast Alaska.

Insight Guides' ***The Pacific Northwest*** covers Northwest history and sights accompanied by many color photographs.

Places to Go with Children by Elton Welke has information about places in the Puget Sound area to explore with children.

The Market Book: A Guide to the Pike Place Market is an in-depth book about the market.

In addition, there are many booklets and other materials put out by groups and areas with information pertaining to their area or activities, such as the ***The Guide to the San Juans*** or ***The Olympic Peninsula***. The local areas' **Chambers of Commerce** and **Visitor Information Centers** are excellent sources for up-to-date information.

The **Seattle Arts Hotline** has recorded phone information on non-profit arts organizations in the Seattle area.

Phone: 447-ARTS.

Index

Maps

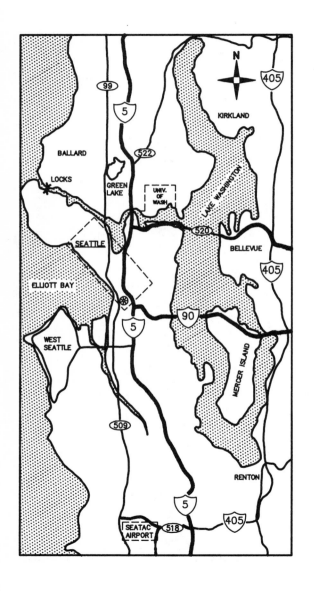

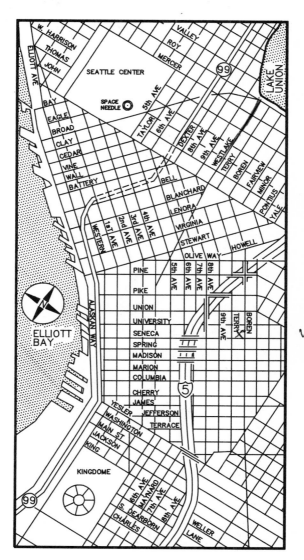

V H